P9-BBT-547

B
WRIGHT

Carson, Mary Kay.

The Wright Brothers
for kids.

44783

$14.95

Brothers for Kids

DATE			

SEDGWICK MIDDLE SCHOOL
LIBRARY MEDIA CENTER
128 SEDGWICK ROAD
WEST HARTFORD, CT 06107

BAKER & TAYLOR

The
Wright Brothers
for Kids

How They Invented the Airplane

*21 Activities Exploring
the Science and History of Flight*

MARY KAY CARSON

CHICAGO
REVIEW
PRESS

44783

Library of Congress Cataloging-in-Publication Data

Carson, Mary Kay.
  The Wright Brothers for kids : how they invented the airplane :
21 activities exploring the science and history of flight / Mary Kay Carson ;
illustrations by Laura D'Argo.— 1st ed.
      p. cm.
  Includes bibliographical references and index.
  ISBN 1-55652-477-3 (alk. paper)
  1. Wright, Orville, 1871–1948—Juvenile literature. 2. Wright, Wilbur,
1867–1912—Juvenile literature. 3. Aeronautics—Experiments—Juvenile
literature. 4. Aeronautics—United States—Biography—Juvenile literature.
I. D'Argo, Laura. II. Title.
TL540.W7C37 2003
629.13'0092'273—dc21   2002155449

The author and the publisher disclaim all liability for use of information contained in this book.

FRONT COVER: Right, courtesy of the Library of Congress, Prints & Photographs Division, LC- W851-129; Top and middle left, courtesy Tom Uhlman; Bottom left, © Corbis.

BACK COVER: Courtesy of the Library of Congress, Prints & Photographs Division: LC-W861-22.

Photographs courtesy of the Library of Congress, Prints & Photographs Division: p. ii, LC-W851-123; p. iii (left), LC-W861-88; p. iii, (right) W861-82; p. xiii, LC-W851-121; p. xiv, LC-W851-65; p. 5, LC-W851-80; p. 6, LC-W851-85; p. 16, LC-W851-82; p. 21 (left), LC-W851-127; p. 28, LC-W851; p. 35 (left), LC-W851-77; p.35 (right), LC-W-851-78; p.36, LC-W851-35; p. 38, LC-W851-73; p. 47, LC-W851-68; p. 51 LC-USZ62-106858; p. 53 (right), LC-W851-83; p. 54, LC-W861-11; p. 57, LC-W851-120, LC-W851-87; p. 60, LC-W851-90; p. 61, LC-W851-97; p. 62, LC-W851-86; p. 63, LC-W851-109; p. 64, LC-W851-85; p.65, LC-W861-120; p. 67, LC-W851-12; p. 70, LC-W851-122; p. 71, LC-W851-111; p. 74, LC-W851-123; p. 79, LC-W861-5; p. 81, LC-W861-1; p. 82, LC-W861-40; p. 83, LC-W861-7; p. 86, LC-W861-61; p. 89, LC-W; p. 89, LC-W861-24; p. 93, LC-W861-16; p. 94, LC-W861-65; p. 97, LC-W851-92; p. 98, LC-W861-19; p.99, LC-W861-35; p. 102 (bottom), LC-W861-22; p. 107 (left), LC-W861-48; p. 109, LC-W861-67; p. 112, LC-W851-129; p. 114, LC-W861-75; p. 116 (left), LC-W861-88; p. 116 (right), LC-W861-82; p. 118, LC-W861-99; p. 122, LC-W861-149; p. 125, LC-W861-95; p. 132, LC-W861-166; p. 134, LC-W861-166; p. 136, LC-W861-24. **Images courtesy of the Library of Congress, Manuscript Division:** p. 53 (left), LC-MSS-15560-1; p. 102 (top), LC-MSS-46706-5. **Photographs are courtesy of Tom Uhlman:** pp. 2, 8, 18, 23, 25, 42, 44, 45, 88, 107 (right), 123, 129, 131, 133, 135, 137. **Photographs taken by Tom Uhlman, courtesy United States Air Force Museum, Wright-Patterson Air For Base, Dayton, Ohio:** pp. 3, 21 (right, statue by James A. Preston), 32, 124, 127, 144; **Tom Uhlman, courtesy Carillon Historical Park:** pp. 10, 17, 76, 96, 106, 108, 110; **Tom Uhlman, courtesy Dayton Heritage National Historic Park, National Park Service:** pp. 11, 13; **Tom Uhlman, *Flyover* sculpture by David Black:** p. 85. **Photograph courtesy of Mark Bowen Photography:** p. 135 (top left).

Cover and interior design: Laura Lindgren Design
Interior illustrations: Laura A. D'Argo
© 2003 by Mary Kay Carson
All rights reserved
First edition
Published by Chicago Review Press, Incorporated
814 North Franklin Street
Chicago, Illinois 60610
ISBN 1-55652-477-3

Printed in China by C & C Offset Company, Ltd.
5 4 3 2 1

To Arthur Bradley, with love

Contents

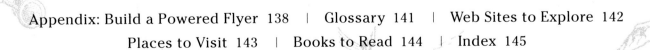

Acknowledgments

A good number of the images in this book were made possible through the generous assistance of the United States Air Force Museum, Wright-Patterson Air Force Base, the Dayton Aviation Heritage National Historical Park, Carillon Historical Park, and the talents of photographer Tom Uhlman. My deepest gratitude to all. A special thanks also to Jerry Pohlen, a patient and supportive editor.

Note to Readers

As well as telling the story of how the Wright brothers invented the airplane, this book features a number of other scientists and inventors who pioneered developments in human flight and early airplanes. To find them, look for the "Early Flight Pioneer" heading throughout the book.

The glossary on page 141 explains the science of flight terms.

Page 143 lists the places pictured in this book (as well as others) that you can visit to see where the Wright brothers lived, worked, and are today commemorated. There is also a list of books to read and videos to watch on page 144, and Web sites to explore on page 142. These will help you learn more about how Wilbur and Orville invented the airplane.

The old-fashioned black-and-white photographs of the Wright brothers, their friends and family, Kitty Hawk, and the gliders and flyers are part of the Wright Brothers Negative Collection of the Library of Congress. Most of the photographs were taken by, or under the direction of, Wilbur and Orville themselves. The Wright brothers believed that photography was a good way to keep a scientific and historical record of their invention. These photographs used glass-plate negatives and many of the negatives have been damaged or broken over the 100 or so years they've been moved, handled, and stored. Some of the negatives were even underwater for several days during Dayton, Ohio's, disastrous 1913 flood.

TIME LINE

1776	U.S. Declaration of Independence
1783	First free balloon flight
1799	Cayley discovers principles of flight
1828	Milton Wright born
1831	Susan Koerner born
1853	First successful fixed-wing glider flight
1865	American Civil War ends
1867	Wilbur Wright born
1871	Orville Wright born Pénaud flies planophore Wenham invents the wind tunnel
1874	Katharine Wright born
1878	Milton Wright brings his sons a toy helicopter
1886	Wilbur seriously injured in accident
1889	Susan Koerner Wright dies Wilbur and Orville start printing business
1892	The Wright Cycle Company formed
1893	Dunbar recites poetry at World's Fair
1894	Chanute's *Progress in Flying Machines* published
1896	Lilienthal dies in gliding accident Chanute tests gliders in Indiana
1899	Wilbur writes to the Smithsonian Wilbur and Orville discover wing warping
1900	Wilbur and Orville test first glider at Kitty Hawk
1901	Wilbur and Orville test second glider at Kitty Hawk Brothers test Lilienthal's tables
1902	Wilbur and Orville test third glider at Kitty Hawk

1903	Langley's Great Aerodrome twice fails to fly
	Wright brothers fly the world's first airplane
1904	Wright brothers move testing to Huffman Prairie
1905	World's first practical airplane, the Wright Flyer III, built
1906	Wright brothers are granted a patent for wing warping
	Santos-Dumont flies the first airplane in Europe
1908	Wilbur flies in Europe
	Orville flies for the U.S. Army and is injured in a crash
	Curtiss makes first public airplane flight in the U.S.
	Ford Model T automobile introduced
1909	Wright Airplane Company formed
	Blériot is first to fly across the English Channel
	Wilbur and Orville welcomed home as heroes
1910	Wilbur and Orville make only flight together
1912	Wilbur Wright dies
1914	World War I breaks out in Europe

1917	Bishop Milton Wright dies
1918	First regular airmail service started by U.S. Army
1920	U.S. women granted right to vote
1924	First round-the-world flight
1928	Lindbergh makes first solo transatlantic flight
1929	Katharine Wright Haskell dies
1932	Wright Brothers National Monument dedicated
	Earhart is first woman to fly solo across the Atlantic
1939	World War II begins
	First jet airplane flight
1947	Yeager is first to fly faster than the speed of sound
1948	Orville Wright dies

Dreams—and Nightmares— of a Flying Machine

The summer was not going well for Wilbur and Orville Wright. The two bicycle makers, brothers from Ohio, had arrived on the North Carolina coast in July after a long train ride, ferry crossing, and boat trip. Kitty Hawk, North Carolina, was not an easy place to get to in 1901. But they'd spent the previous summer there testing a glider in the strong wind with some success. And they'd wanted to come back to do the same with the newly designed glider they'd spent the winter building in Ohio. The new 22-foot-wide (6.7-m) glider had much better wing controls for the pilot than the previous model. It would be the biggest glider ever flown! Surely it would fly better and farther than last year's glider.

Unfortunately bad weather arrived with the Wright brothers at Kitty Hawk. Heavy rain drenched the beach and the Wright brothers' camp for an entire week. The winds constantly whipped around wet stinging sand. When the rain finally let up, a plague of mosquitoes moved in. "The sand and grass and trees and hills and everything was fairly covered with them," Orville wrote to his sister Katharine back home in Dayton. "They chewed us clear through our underwear and socks. Lumps began swelling up all over my body like hen's eggs." Orville and Wilbur were soon ill from the weather and insect bites.

When the brothers were finally able to put their new glider together and get started trying it out, things only got worse. The new glider just wouldn't fly as it was supposed to. The wings didn't seem to lift the glider high up into the air as they should based on the brothers' careful design. And the new system of wing controls wasn't working either. When Wilbur tried to steer the glider, it would sometimes spin out of control. In fact, the glider was turning out to be dangerous. One day as Wilbur flew over the sand, the glider's left wing dipped. When Wilbur used the controls to try to level out the glider, it crashed into the sand. The glider's front was badly smashed and so was Wilbur. He had a black eye, bruised nose, and cuts on his face. The brothers didn't make many more glides after fixing the glider. They went back to flying it attached to ropes like a kite.

When rains returned in August, Orville and Wilbur gave up and started packing. What was the point of staying? They hadn't built a bigger, better glider—they'd just discovered a whole world of new problems. They left their Kitty Hawk camp in late August and went home. When they got back to Dayton, Wilbur went straight to bed, sick with a cold and depressed. "We doubted that we would ever resume our experiments," wrote Wilbur later. Building a successful flying machine felt like a mountain they could never hope to climb. They'd already worked so hard, for so long, and spent so much money! Wilbur declared to Orville, "Not within a thousand years will man ever fly!"

The Wright brothers flying the 1901 glider as a kite.

Wilbur Wright was wrong. Human flight was two years—not a thousand—away. And it would be the Wright brothers who would make it happen. Within a year the brothers solved the wing and control problems and built a successful glider. The year after that, they added an engine attached to propellers and flew the first powered, piloted, heavier-than-air flying machine. How did these two bicycle makers with no college education and no financial backing do it? How did the Wright brothers invent the airplane?

ONE

Bishops, Boys, and Bicycles

Wilbur and Orville's mother had good news for her two youngest sons. "Your father will be home from his business trip today, boys!" Susan Wright happily announced. At 11 years old, Wilbur understood that his father had to spend a lot of time away from home visiting other towns and cities on church business. After all, Milton Wright was now a bishop in the United Brethren Church. His election to bishop was why the family had moved to Iowa earlier in the year. At only seven years old, Orville also knew his father was an important man in the church. But he was always excited when his father came back home. Especially when he brought the boys presents from his travels!

Orville and Wilbur weren't disappointed when their father arrived at the house. He was holding a surprise hidden in his cupped hands. "Look at this, boys!" Bishop Wright exclaimed as he tossed

← The Wright family home at 7 Hawthorn Street in Dayton, Ohio.

the gift toward Orville and Wilbur. The brothers rushed forward to catch their present. But the tossed toy instead rose up into the air. Orville and Wilbur stood with their mouths open watching as the miraculous toy flew up to the ceiling, fluttered for a while suspended in midair, and then fell to the floor. Oh my, but it was grand! They ran to examine it up close.

Bishop Wright had brought his sons a toy flying machine made of cork, lightweight bamboo wood, and thin paper. The toy was powered by twisted rubber bands attached to two propellers stacked one over the other. In those days, toys that flew by spinning up into the air were called Chinese flying tops. Most were operated by means of a string wrapped around them, like a top. When pulled, the string would send the toy spinning upward. Chinese flying tops had been around for centuries. But the version that Milton Wright likely paid about a half dollar for was the latest model from France. It was sold as a toy, but a serious student of flight named Alphonse Pénaud had designed it. Its rubber bands made it a true powered flying machine, called a hélicoptère.

Wilbur and Orville flew the rubber–band powered helicopter, which they called "the bat," again and again. The bat could fly up to 50 feet (15 m) in the air! They played with it until the fragile toy fell apart. Then older brother Wilbur built new ones by copying the toy's construction.

Spinning helicopter toys are still around today.

ALPHONSE PÉNAUD
(1850–1880)

The flying helicopter that Bishop Wright gave Wilbur and Orville was designed by a young Frenchman named Alphonse Pénaud. What the Wright boys called a bat was sold as a toy, but it was really a model powered flying machine. (You can build your own rubber band–powered flying machine by following the directions on page 138.)

Pénaud, the son of an admiral, planned to follow his father into the French navy. But a crippling hip disease confined him to a wheelchair at a young age. Unable to live a life at sea, Pénaud turned his imagination to the sky. He began experimenting with flight by building models that were powered in an ingenious way. Pénaud used twisted strands of elastic–rubber bands. The propellers were made of paper and some small parts out of lightweight aluminum. In 1871 Pénaud flew his model powered glider (not a helicopter) a distance of more than 60 feet (18 m). Today, we'd call his planophore a model airplane.

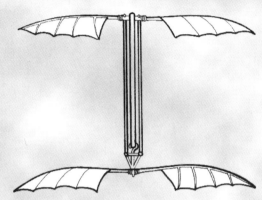

Pénaud's Héliocoptère

Pénaud studied the work of Sir George Cayley (see "Father of Aerial Navigation" on page 34) and conducted his own experiments with his planophore. He studied how to make it fly steady and stable by changing the shape of the wings and tail. Pénaud also did experiments and wrote scientific papers about how air moves around a flying machine. In 1875, the French Academy of Sciences awarded him a prize for his work.

Just a few years after Orville was born, Pénaud got a patent on a full-size airplane design. He spent four years trying to find the money to build his flying machine. But no one would fund him. Depressed and in poor health, Pénaud tragically took his own life at age 30.

This replica of the Pénaud planophore is on display at the United States Air Force Museum.

After a while, Wilbur decided he wanted a bat that could fly farther and stay up in the air longer. So he tried to build a bigger one. But to the boys' amazement, a bigger bat didn't fly farther—it barely flew at all!

Will and Orv, as they were known, lost interest in bat building after a while and eventually gave up trying to build a bigger one. At eleven and seven years old they had other things to do, after all. Wilbur liked to play sports and Orville was always busy leading his army of friends on neighborhood marches. But their father's gift had sparked the boys' imagination. Later in his life Orville Wright wrote that he and his brother's lifelong interest in flying began with the toy.

Milton's and Susan's Family

Wilbur and Orville were given the bat when they lived in Cedar Rapids, Iowa. It was one of a half dozen places they lived in Iowa, Indiana, and Ohio as children. The family moved around so much because their father, Milton Wright, was a minister—and eventually a bishop—in the United Brethren Church. He was born in 1828 and raised in a log cabin in frontier Indiana. His great-great-great grandfather was a Puritan who came from England soon after the *Mayflower* landed at Plymouth Rock, and his great grandmother was the first white woman to set foot in Dayton, Ohio. Milton left the family farm as a young man, went to college, and became a teacher and minister. The United Brethren Church sent young Milton to Oregon in the 1850s on church business. Oregon wasn't an easy place to get to in those days! Milton Wright had to travel to the East Coast by train, take one boat all the way to Central America, cross Panama by train, take a boat to San Francisco and another one to the Oregon coast before heading inland.

When he returned home from Oregon, Milton Wright married Susan Koerner in Indiana. Susan was the daughter of a German-born wheelwright. While growing up Susan spent a lot of time in her father's Hillsboro, Indiana, shop where he made carriages and wagons. Susan learned to use tools, make and repair things with her hands, and figure out how machines worked. These were skills she passed on to her children. Susan Koerner also attended college, something quite rare for women in Indiana in the 1850s. It was at Hartsville College that Susan met her future husband.

By the standards of the time, Susan and Milton Wright married and started a family late in life. Their first child, a son named Reuchlin, was born in 1861, the year the American Civil War began, when Susan was nearly 30 years old. A second son, Lorin, was born during the war. Reverend Milton Wright was, like all United Brethren, a pacifist. He did not believe in war so he did not join the army to fight against the Confederates nor would he preach to soldiers. However, Milton Wright was an outspoken abolitionist, and he hoped that the war would forever end the shame of slavery.

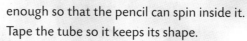

Fly a Top

The young Wright brothers were fascinated by a popular toy of the time called a Chinese flying top, even before their father gave them the more sophisticated bat. These simple helicopter spinners had a propeller on the top and would fly when a string was pulled. You can build your own flying top and watch it spin up into the air.

You'll Need
3 feet (1 m) of thick thread or thin string
Empty plastic bottle (soda bottle or laundry
    detergent bottle works well)
Piece of lightweight cardboard roughly
    2 inches by 3 inches (5 cm by 7.5 cm), the
    thickness of a cereal box or poster board
Pencil with eraser
Thumbtack
Ruler
Permanent marker
Tape
Scissors

1. Wrap the cardboard rectangle around the pencil lengthwise to make a tube. The tube should be loose enough so that the pencil can spin inside it. Tape the tube so it keeps its shape.

2. Use the ruler and marker to draw a rectangle that measures 5 inches by ½ inch (12.7 cm by 1.3 cm) on a flat part of the plastic bottle. Carefully cut out the rectangle, or ask an adult to cut it out. This is the propeller.

3. Find the midpoint of the propeller. Draw lines connecting the opposite corners. Where they cross is the midpoint.

4. Push the thumbtack through the midpoint of the propeller. Grab both ends of the propeller and twist it. The right side bends upward and the left side bends down, as shown.

5. Attach the propeller to the top of the pencil by pushing the thumbtack into the eraser. If the propeller slides around between the thumbtack and the eraser, wrap a piece of tape over them to hold it secure. (This looseness might not happen until after you've flown it a couple of times.)

6. Start wrapping the string around the pencil about halfway up. Wrap the string up the pencil tightly and smoothly. Leave about 2 to 3 inches (5 to 7.5 cm) of unwrapped string at the top. This is the pull end.

7. Put the pencil inside the cardboard tube while carefully holding onto the pull end of the string. Gently hold the tube in one hand and pull the string with the other. Pull quickly, with force, but smoothly. Watch your top fly!

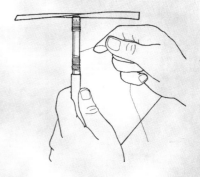

Parlor of the Wright family home at 7 Hawthorn Street.

a seminary. But Milton Wright was becoming an important man in his church, and the leaders wanted him to edit their influential newspaper in Dayton, Ohio. The family moved again.

Twins named Ida and Otis were born to the Wrights in Dayton, but sadly both died before reaching their first birthday. The family moved into a house at 7 Hawthorn Street in Dayton when Susan Wright was 4 months pregnant with Orville. The house on Hawthorn Street would become the Wright family home and would later be moved to a museum. Orville was born in the upstairs front bedroom at the Hawthorn Street house on August 19, 1871. His little sister Katharine, the youngest and final Wright child, was born exactly three years later to the day.

Preacher's Kids

Not long after the end of the Civil War and the assassination of President Abraham Lincoln, the Wrights moved to a small farm in Millville, Indiana. A couple of years later, on April 16, 1867, they had a third son, Wilbur. Like his brothers before him, he wasn't given an "unnecessary" middle name and was named after an admired clergyman. The year after Wilbur's birth, the family moved back to Hartsville, where Reverend Wright founded

Wilbur and Orville grew up like most other boys in midwestern towns during the late 1800s. Their modest neighborhood in West Dayton was home to carpenters, salesmen, wagon makers, and book-keepers who rode streetcars downtown to work. Wilbur and Orville Wright went to school and played with friends as all kids do. But everyday life was very different back then. The Hawthorn Street house stood on a small lot without much yard. While there were bedrooms upstairs and a kitchen, dining room, and sitting room down-stairs, the bathroom was an outhouse behind

Ten-year-old Wilbur Wright.

the house. Any water used in the house had to be brought in from a pump outside the kitchen door. There was no electricity or radio—and of course no television, video games, or computers. Lamps filled with oil provided light, and coal fueled a heater during the winter. Susan Wright cooked for her large family on a wood-burning stove in the kitchen. People traveled by streetcar, train, horse-drawn carriage, or on foot. Automobiles were unheard-of back then. It's amazing to think that boys who grew up without cars, indoor plumbing, or electricity would one day invent the airplane.

From the outside, Wilbur and Orville seemed like ordinary boys growing up in an average family. But they actually had quite out-of-the-ordinary parents for their day. Both Susan and Milton Wright

had been to college, traveled, and taught school before marrying. They both had a lot of knowledge and experience, which they delighted in sharing with their children. Reverend Wright had a library of books, which he encouraged his children to read. As a United Brethren minister, Milton Wright was a nondrinker and disallowed card playing as a waste of time. But he believed in equal opportunity for women long before women had voting rights. He sent his daughter to college and allowed his children to read books that disagreed with his own religious beliefs.

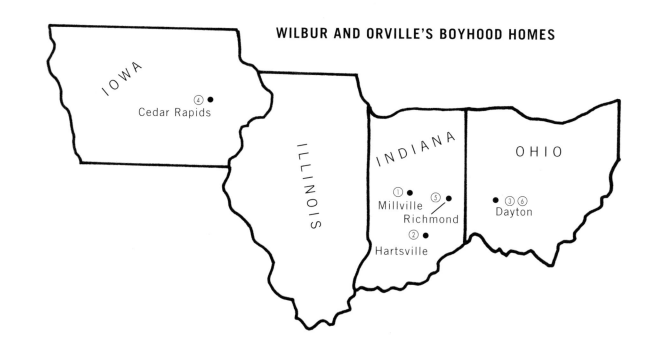

WILBUR AND ORVILLE'S BOYHOOD HOMES

1 Wilbur is born in Millville, Indiana, in 1867.
2 Family moves down to Hartsville in 1868.
3 Wrights move to Dayton, Ohio, in 1870, where Orville is born in 1871.
4 Family moves to Cedar Rapids, Iowa, in 1878.
5 Wrights move to a farm near Richmond, Indiana, in 1881.
6 Family returns to Dayton, Ohio, in 1884.

Quick Kite

Kite flying was a popular pastime in the 1800s and Wilbur and Orville built and flew kites as children. Little did they know that they'd fly kites as adults, too! You can easily give kite flying a try by making this super simple kite that only takes minutes to put together. If you discover you like kite flying, try the more complex kite on page 14 next.

You'll Need
8½-inch by 11-inch (22-cm by 28-cm) sheet of
   paper (thinner is better)
8-inch (20-cm) plastic drinking straw or
   bamboo skewer
10-foot (3-m) lightweight tail made of plastic
   flagging tape, paper party streamer cut in
   half lengthwise, or a spiral cut out of a
   plastic bag
1-inch by 3-inch (2.5-cm by 7.5-cm) piece of
   heavy cardboard or a toilet tissue tube
Ruler
Pencil or pen
10 to 15 feet (3 to 5 m) of lightweight string,
   or kite string
Scissors
Hole punch or sharpened pencil

1. Fold the sheet of paper in half crosswise and leave it folded.
2. Use the ruler to measure 1½ inches (3.8 cm) in from the crease on the top edge and put an X there. Use the ruler to measure 4½ inches (11.4 cm) in from the crease on the bottom edge and put an X there. Use the ruler to draw a line connecting the Xs, as shown.

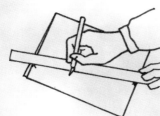

3. Fold back the top layer of paper along the line and crease it.

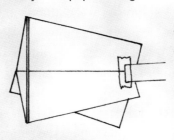

Put tape all along the crease. Tape the straw (or bamboo skewer) down across the widest part of the front and tape the tail to the small end, as shown.

4. Turn the kite over. Crease both sides until the middle folded section stands up on its own. Cover the narrow end of the middle folded section with some tape on both sides. This will keep the hole from tearing. Use a hole punch or a pencil tip to put a hole in this end.

5. Put one end of the string through this hole and tie it. Wind the rest of the string around the cardboard piece or tube.

6. Fly it! On a breezy day unravel some of the string and stand with your back to the wind. Walk quickly backward until the wind catches the kite and flings it up into the air. Keep the string tight by gently tugging down on it.

BE SAFE: Choose a wide, open area away from power lines and busy streets to fly your kite. Never fly a kite in a thunderstorm. Never try to retrieve a kite stuck in a tree or in power lines!

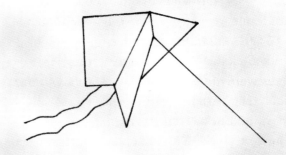

Milton Wright encouraged his children to believe in themselves and think for themselves. The toy helicopter wasn't the only educational toy the Wright children would receive. In fact, Orville was given a spinning gyroscope for his fifth birthday. Their father was away from home a lot, but he constantly wrote detailed letters describing the faraway places he saw. The bishop's descriptions of Native Americans living in Montana and colorful California fairs opened a world unknown to other children in the Wrights' Dayton neighborhood.

The Wright children were expected to write letters to their father while he was away from home and they did so from a young age. In a letter Orville wrote to his father at age nine, he describes an experiment he did in the kitchen. "The other day I took a machine can and filled it with water then I put it on the stove. I waited a little while and the water came squirting out of the top about a foot." Apparently Susan Wright didn't mind science experiments in her kitchen! That's not really surprising. She was said to be able to fix and build all sorts of useful household tools and appliances. Susan Wright even crafted a sled for her kids. When Will and Orv needed advice on how to work something or how to fix it, they went to their mother for help. She gave the boys their uncanny ability to see in their heads how something would work—before they built it.

Orville realized that their upbringing had been very special, later saying, "We were lucky enough to grow up in an environment where there was always much encouragement to children to pursue intellectual interest; to investigate whatever aroused curiosity. In a different kind of environment, our curiosity might have been nipped long before it could have borne fruit."

Coming of Age

Wilbur and Orville grew up in a close-knit family. Wilbur taught his kid brother Orville how to build and fly kites and told him stories. But because the boys were four years apart, they naturally had different friends and different interests as kids. Orville was a baby brother to teenage Wilbur, a quiet, thoughtful young man who loved to read and was an excellent student bound for college. After the family moved from Iowa to a farm in Indiana, Wilbur enrolled in honors classes at Richmond High School. Wilbur was very athletic and loved to play sports. He was good at gymnastics and rode a high-wheeler bicycle. Wilbur also helped out at his father's church newspaper as a teenager. Wilbur's job was to fold the newspapers so they could be mailed. It was boring work, so Wilbur invented a machine that folded the papers quicker using a foot pedal!

Meanwhile, Orville was a rambunctious kid who played army with his friends, adored his baby sister, and was always cooking up some money-making scheme. He did well enough in school, but he wasn't an overachiever. Apparently he played hooky his entire first month of kindergarten. Instead of heading to school after leaving

Today kites come in all sorts of shapes and sizes.

the house each morning, he went straight to his neighbor and friend Ed Sines's house to play with an old sewing machine! Orville had a reputation, and teachers often made him sit in the front row where they could keep an eye on him. The youngest Wright son seemed more interested in making pocket money than studying. His parents thought he'd end up in business, not college. Orville took to designing, making, and selling kites at age 12 and became known as quite an expert kite maker in the neighborhood. While in Richmond, Orville also collected scrap metal and bones for money, tried (but failed) to invent a sugared chewing gum, and even organized a circus.

The Wrights had moved to Richmond in part because their mother had become ill with tuberculosis, a disease of the lungs. At the time it was an incurable disease that killed many people all over the world. Tuberculosis sufferers coughed, had trouble breathing, and over time became weaker and sicker. Richmond, Indiana, was near Susan Wright's childhood home, and nearby family helped out when her husband went on his long trips. For the boys, one great benefit of being back in Indiana was spending time at Grandfather Koerner's farm. Wilbur and Orville loved to explore the carriage and wagon shop, tinkering with the woodworking machines and wheelwright tools. It was there that the brothers built their first machine together. It was a six-foot lathe, a tool for carving wood. A foot pedal, called a treadle, powered the machine. Wilbur even had the idea of making ball bearings with marbles housed in some discarded metal rings from a horse harness.

In 1884 the Wrights left Indiana and moved back to Dayton, Ohio. Bishop Wright's church wanted him back near its headquarters. It was the twelfth time in her 25 years of marriage that Susan Wright had moved her household, husband, and children. Now a sickly woman of 53 years, she dutifully packed up her family and their belongings and loaded them onto the Dayton train. It would turn out to be her final move.

Wilbur was now nearly 18 and taking classes to prepare himself for Yale University. He also played football for Central High and was known as one of the school's fastest runners. But Wilbur's plans for college and his robust health both came to an end one cold winter day. He and some friends were playing shinny on a frozen lake. It's a game similar to hockey. Players wear ice skates and use heavy sticks to move a ball or puck around. A player accidentally hit Wilbur in the face with a shinny stick. He was violently knocked to the ground. The blow knocked out all his upper front teeth and some lower ones, too. After a number of dental operations, Wilbur also started having odd problems with his heart as well. His recovery took so long that he began to doubt whether his health would ever fully return. He worried that a college education might be wasted on someone who could so easily become bedridden. How could be become a teacher or scientist if he was always going to be ill? Feeling hopeless and defeated, Wilbur fell into a long, deep depression.

While at home trying to recover his own health and rediscover happiness, Wilbur took care of his mother. Susan Wright's tuberculosis was worsening every year. She was now unable to leave the house or care for herself. While Wilbur looked after his dying mother, Bishop Wright continued to travel on church business. Wilbur spent those years reading and studying, too. Nursing his mother made him feel important, useful, and needed. Working his way through his father's library of encyclopedias, biographies, and books about history, science, and religion became the college education Wilbur would never receive. Learning about the world through books and expertly caring for his mother helped build back Wilbur's confidence in himself, the world, and his place in it. By his 21st birthday, Wilbur's depression was lifting and he began helping his father write for church publications.

Meanwhile, young Orville was busy becoming a printer. When the family had returned to Dayton, Orville had taken up with his old friend and partner in childhood crime, Ed Sines, who happened to have a toy printing setup. Ed and Orville soon acquired somewhat better equipment and were in business trying to print a small newspaper for their eighth-grade classmates. Because the printer could only print on small sheets of paper, the newspaper was called *The Midget*. Soon Sines & Wright was printing cards, tickets, envelopes, and handbills for local businesses. During the summers of his high school years, Orville added to his skills by apprenticing at a local printing shop. Wilbur pitched in and helped when his kid brother struggled to build his first professional press. They ended up using an old gravestone, hinges from the folding top of a horse buggy, and scrap metal. When a printer who'd heard about the homemade press came to see it, he remarked, "It works all right, but I still don't understand *why* it works." Orville and Ed Sines put their odd press to work writing and printing a newspaper, the *West Side News*. A six-week subscription cost 10 cents. Orville didn't plan on going back for his last year of high school. He was happy being a successful printer.

Tuberculosis finally took the life of Susan Koerner Wright. She died on Independence Day in 1889. Wilbur was now 22 and beyond the age when most young men started college. While he had spent the last few years caring for his mother and studying his father's library, his kid brother Orville had grown up and learned a trade. They were still brothers, but no longer boys. The age difference that had seemed so great when they were children was less and less noticeable as they became men. Orville asked Wilbur to join him in the printing business. Wilbur soon became the editor and Orville the publisher of the *West Side News*. The newspaper wouldn't last long, but the brothers' business partnership would. In fact, it was to be a lifetime partnership that would go down in history.

The March 1, 1889, issue of the *West Side News*. Look for Orville's name as publisher in the top left-hand corner.

PAUL LAURENCE DUNBAR

(1872–1906)

Orville Wright wasn't the only Dayton Central High School student to become famous. The African American poet Paul Laurence Dunbar and Orville were classmates. Unlike Orville, Dunbar was a very good student. He was also editor of the school paper.

Dunbar's parents were born slaves. His father escaped from slavery and fought for the Union in the American Civil War. Encouraged by his mother, who taught him a love for songs, poems, and storytelling, Dunbar began writing his own poems as a young child. After high school, he decided to try to publish a newsletter for Dayton's African American community. His friend Orville Wright now had a printing business, Wright & Wright, and agreed to print the newsletter. So Dunbar wrote and edited the *Dayton Tattler*. But he had trouble selling advertisements for the newsletter, and soon ran out of money. It was during the *Dayton Tattler*'s six-week run that Dunbar apparently wrote these lines on the print shop wall:

> Orville Wright is out of sight
> In the printing business.
> No other mind is half so bright
> As his'n is.

Even though the *Dayton Tattler* failed, Dunbar kept writing poems and eventually began reading them for audiences. The publishing house of Bishop Wright's United Brethren Church printed 500 copies of Paul Laurence Dunbar's first book of poems, *Oak and Ivy*. In 1893 Dunbar was invited to recite his poems at the World's Fair. Dunbar's poems made him one of the most popular American poets of the 1890s and early 1900s. In his short life, he published twelve books of poetry, four books of short stories, a play, and five novels. No other African American writer would publish as many works until 1950.

Paul Laurence Dunbar

At the age of 18, Paul Laurence Dunbar began a newspaper for African Americans, the *Dayton Tattler*. Wilbur and Orville, Paul's classmate, printed the paper at their Hoover Block print shop.

Dunbar went on to achieve international fame as a poet, author, lyricist, and powerful reader of verse. He set one of his novels and several short stories in fictional Ohio towns that resembled Dayton. Dunbar returned to Dayton in 1903 and purchased a comfortable brick home on the West Side. He died there of tuberculosis at age 33.

This Paul Laurence Dunbar display is part of the Dayton Aviation Heritage National Historical Park.

The Merry Wheel

The *West Side News* and another newspaper the brothers started, the *Evening Item*, couldn't really compete with the big Dayton newspapers. The Wright brothers got out of the newspaper business less than two years after they got in. They decided to concentrate on printing things for other businesses and individuals instead. The printing company of Wright & Wright printed all sorts of things for its customers—posters, business cards, church and club directories, reports for businesses and state offices, and sale flyers for stores. But the truth was that the brothers were getting a bit bored with printing. Once the business was up and running, Ed Sines handled a lot of the day-to-day work. And with no newspapers to write or edit, Wilbur felt there wasn't much for him to do at Wright & Wright. Orville and Wilbur began to think about what they could do for a new—more interesting—business enterprise.

The second half of the 1800s was a time of great change in how Americans went about their

---

A C T I V I T Y

Neighborhood News

In 1889 the Wright brothers began publishing a weekly newspaper called the *West Side News*. Orville was the publisher and Wilbur the editor. Orville's friend Ed Sines gathered news and stories in their Dayton neighborhood, Wilbur decided which stories would be printed, and Orville printed the newspaper. Writing and publishing your own family or neighborhood newspaper can be a lot of fun!

You'll Need
Paper
Pens
Photocopier

1. Make a plan. Think about:
   What will your newspaper cover—your family, your apartment building, your block?
   What do you want in the paper—news stories about what people are doing, ideas for fun things to do nearby, movie reviews, cartoons, photos?
   How long will it be—one side of one page, two sides, many pages?
2. Gather up what you want to go into the newspaper. Write up the news stories, movie reviews, and events listings, and get the pictures together.

3. Lay out your copy on sheets of paper. You can handwrite the stories around pictures or use a typewriter or computer and then cut out and paste the text and graphics onto the pages.
4. Photocopy the pages and distribute your newspaper!

This Wright Cycle Company shop was used by the brothers from 1895 to 1897 and is now part of the Dayton Aviation Heritage National Historical Park.

daily lives. Ordinary people who, like Will and Orv, had grown up with outhouses and homes lit by oil lamps, watched as houses were wired for electricity and installed with indoor water pipes and toilets. The telephone, lightbulb, phonograph, and other inventions by men such as Alexander Graham Bell and Thomas Edison amazed everyone. How people got from place to place was also quickly changing. Steam engines powered trains, ships, and factories during the 1800s. But getting around town meant walking, waiting for a street-car, or taking a horse-drawn carriage. Toward the very end of the century people were building horseless carriages powered by gasoline engines, but the automobile would be beyond the means of most Americans for many years.

It was the bicycle that became America's first personal vehicle. Bicycles of the old-fashioned high-wheeler sort had been around since the Wright brothers were boys. As a teenager in Richmond, Indiana, Wilbur had owned one of the contraptions with its giant front wheel, tiny back wheel, and solid tires. But high-wheelers were difficult to ride and easy to wreck. Riding them was a dangerous sport, not an easy way to get around. The arrival of a newly invented bicycle from Europe in 1887 changed all that. The easy-to-ride safety bicycle had two equal-size wheels, air-filled rubber tires, and hand brakes. (See photo on p. 17.)

Bicycling quickly became a popular pastime. Millions of Americans bought bicycles and rode them everywhere. Bicycles were called the greatest invention of the 19th century. They were affordable. A person could ride a bicycle to and from work or school and get there faster than a horse-drawn carriage. People could ride their bikes to visit friends or relatives without waiting for a train or walking for miles. Young Americans accustomed to wearing stiff high collars and tight corsets, long skirts, and wool suits were now peddling around town on bicycles with friends. They felt a new sense of independence and freedom. Speeding downhill into the wind was the closest thing to flying—and Wilbur and Orville Wright loved it.

Orville and Wilbur bought bikes in 1892 and joined the craze that hit Dayton that year. Their friend Ed Sines and some other men organized cycle clubs, races, and group bicycle trips. Wilbur liked to go on long bicycle rides in the country, while Orville loved to race on a track against other riders. Becoming bicycle mechanics was inevitable for the Wright brothers. Everyone in the neighborhood knew that the brothers were handy with machines and that they'd built their own printing press. Friends started showing up at the print shop with broken bikes to be fixed, and word soon spread. The new—more interesting—business enterprise that the Wright brothers had been looking for had found them.

Wright Cycle Exchange

Orville and Wilbur rented a storefront and set up shop repairing and selling bicycles in 1893. The

Curved Kite

While Wilbur gave up kite flying as a teenager, Orville put his kite-building skills to work. To earn spending money, Orville built and sold kites to neighborhood kids. He discovered that the thinner he'd make the kite frames' wooden strips, the better the kites flew. This was because the thinner strips bent and made a curved flying surface. It was information the brothers would use as adults when building gliders. You can build your own kite that has a curved surface by following these instructions.

You'll Need

2 to 4 millimeter-thick disposable plastic tarp

3 wooden dowels, each 29 inches (74 cm) long and 1/8 inch (3 mm) thick

2-inch (5-cm) clear plastic packaging tape

6-foot (2-m) length of fishing line

Kite string

Hole punch or nail

Small fishing swivel

Yardstick

Scissors

Permanent marker

10-foot (3-m) lightweight tail made of plastic flagging tape, paper party streamer, or a spiral cut out of a plastic bag (optional)

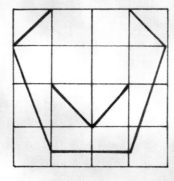

1. Use a marker and yardstick to measure and cut a 32-inch by 32-inch (80-cm by 80-cm) square out of the tarp. Draw a grid of 8-inch (20-cm) squares. You should have four rows and four columns.

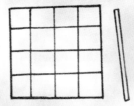

2. Cut off three inches of the bottom row. You now have a 32-inch by 29-inch (80-cm by 75-cm) rectangle. Using the grid lines and the diagram as a guide, cut off the four corners of the rectangle. This is the outline of the kite.

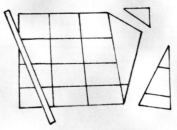

3. Again using the grid lines and the diagram as a guide, completely cut out the triangular vent.

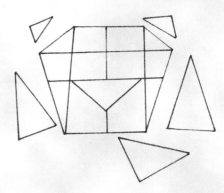

4. Take the three wooden dowels and lay them on the three 8-inch (20-cm) vertical grid lines. Use small pieces of the plastic packing tape to secure the ends of the dowels to the edges of the kite fabric by wrapping the tape over the edges.

5. Use more small pieces of the plastic packing tape to tape the dowels to the rest of the kite

plastic. Pay special attention to taping the dowels to the areas around the open vent. Any tape beyond the outline of the kite can easily be trimmed away.

6. Cover the two outermost corners of the kite where it's widest with a fold of packing tape. This will make the corners stronger. Use the hole punch or a nail to poke holes in these corners on the grid line about an inch (2.5 cm) from the edge. Trim the extra tape away, so the corners keep their shape.

7. Take the fishing line, fold it in half, and mark its midpoint with the marker. Tie the fishing

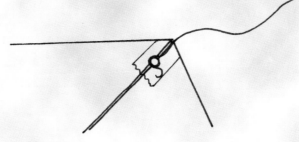

swivel into the line where you marked it. Tie each end of the fishing line to each of the holes on the sides of the kite.

8. Tie the end of your kite string to the fishing swivel. You can add a tail if you like. Use the packing tape to secure the tail to the bottom of the kite. (You might try flying it both with and without the tail and see which is better, depending on how windy it is.)

9. Fly it! On a breezy day unravel some of the string and stand with your back to the wind. Walk quickly backward until the wind catches the kite and flings it up into the air. Keep the line taut!

BE SAFE: Choose a wide, open area away from power lines and busy streets to fly your kite. Never fly a kite in a thunderstorm! Never try to retrieve a kite stuck in a tree or in power lines!

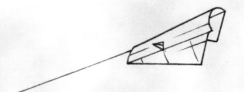

Wright Cycle Exchange carried the best bicycle brands on the market—brands such as Fleetwing, Warwick, and Coventry. Bicycles weren't cheap and the brothers allowed their customers to make payments over time, in the same way most people buy a car today. They also took trade-ins, sold parts, and rented bicycles. The business did well and the brothers soon moved to a larger store and renamed their enterprise the Wright Cycle Company.

After a couple of years of repairing and selling bicycles made by others, the Wright brothers decided that they could build a better bicycle themselves. The bicycle business was very slow during the winter, so why not spend that time building their own bicycles? The brothers went to work turning the upstairs of their store into a machine shop. They built an engine that ran on city gas to power the drill press, lathe, and steel tube cutting tools. They fashioned electrical welding equipment and designed improved brakes and wheels for their custom-built bicycle models for men, women, and children. The bicycles sold for between about $20 and $65, reasonable prices at the time.

Setting up a bicycle-making operation was a big job, but it was a fun challenge for Wilbur and Orville. Little did they know that building bicycles was actually perfect training for someday building the world's first airplane. Today we think of bikes as simple machines. But when it was invented, the bicycle was the most high-tech vehicle around. It was made not of old-fashioned iron and wood but of new materials such as steel and rubber. Bicycle production required welding with electricity, precision cutting of chains and gears, and tools powered by small efficient engines. In fact, an article in a New York newspaper of the day eerily predicted that it would be bicycle makers who would someday invent a flying machine. Who else was more qualified to build a machine that flew than those already making the lightest and swiftest machines around? And didn't riding a bike feel like flying?

Making and selling their own brand of bicycles kept the Wright brothers busy and earned them a good living. But with the shop up and running smoothly, it was no longer enough of a challenge to hold all of their interest. Wilbur had never really wanted to be a businessman, after all, and he doubted that he'd ever become anyone important in the business world. "I might make a living but I doubt whether I would ever do much more than this," Wilbur wrote his father,

Orville Wright and Ed Sines working in the back of the Wright bicycle shop. Look for the bike frames on the right and the bike parts hanging on the wall.

who was again away on church business. Wilbur was thinking of going to college. "Intellectual effort is a pleasure to me and I think I would be better fitted for reasonable success in some of the professions [rather] than in business." Wilbur was nearly 30 and he worried that, like his two older brothers Lorin and Reuchlin, he wasn't living up to his potential. He wrote in a letter that none of the boys of the Wright family "has as yet made particular use of the talent in which he excels other men." Only their baby sister Katharine had made it to college. Wilbur desperately wanted to make his mark on the world—but how?

Meanwhile Orville was starting to become interested in the next wave in personal transportation that was just coming on the scene. A friend who worked at the Wright Cycle Company, Cordy

Ruse, built Dayton's first automobile in 1896. Orville liked to help Cordy tinker with his noisy, sputtering, rattling machine and he thought that perhaps the Wright brothers should go into business building their own horseless carriages. Orville suspected that horseless carriages would become popular and might even someday replace bicycles! Wilbur thought otherwise. Turning a noisy, dirty, and unreliable early automobile design into a practical way to get around would be "tackling the impossible," said Wilbur. "Why, it would be easier to build a flying machine!"

Old-fashioned bicycles on display at Carillon Historical Park in Dayton, Ohio. The bike on the right is a high-wheeler and the one on the left is an early safety bicycle.

TWO

First Thoughts of Flight

In the 1890s there was no radio, television, or Internet. The Wright family depended on newspapers and magazines to learn about what was happening in the outside world. Dayton was now a small city proud of its 12 miles (19 km) of paved road, sewer lines, and 11-story "skyscraper." When Wilbur and Orville weren't making bicycles, they especially liked to read about any new inventions or technologies that the new breed of engineers—and wacky cranks—was working on.

Late in the summer of 1896 Orville came down with typhoid. The disease had no treatment at the time and often could be fatal. Typhoid was spread mostly through contaminated drinking water. Bishop Wright ordered the well outside the bike shop where the brothers pumped their water sealed off. Poor Orville lay in bed for weeks delirious with fever. He very nearly died. It would be more than a month before Orville would be able to even sit up in bed. His brother and business partner Wilbur spent many hours at his bedside reading to him, even when he wasn't sure if Orville could hear him. It was most likely during these weeks that Wilbur read (and read to Orville) about the death of the Flying Man.

Otto Lilienthal (see page 20) was a German engineer who had become famous for strapping himself into what looked like giant bat wings, jumping off high hills, and flying. Lilienthal was actually gliding. He didn't flap the wings or power them in any way. Today we'd call what he did hang gliding. From 1891 to 1896, Otto Lilienthal made the first successful piloted glider flights. While others before him had flown in gliders, Lilienthal was the first to control, or pilot, a glider. He changed the glider's direction by swinging his legs, which dangled below, back and forth. This shifted his weight. Unfortunately, controlling a

← Turkey vultures soaring with ease.

glider like this wasn't easy. While he was gliding in 1896, a wind gust crashed his glider and killed him. Lilienthal's final words were, "Sacrifices must be made."

Orville fully recovered from typhoid and the Wright brothers went back to work making bicycles. But Lilienthal's deadly accident stayed on their minds and they talked about it a lot. The brothers had been fascinated with flying machines since their father had given them the helicopter toy. And Lilienthal's attempts had been in the news over the past few years. Wilbur and Orville had seen a magazine article that had newfangled photographs of Lilienthal gliding. Wilbur and Orville had even reported on one of Lilienthal's early attempts at flight in their short-lived newspaper, the *Evening Item*, a few years back. But now the Flying Man was dead. Why did he crash? Lilienthal had made thousands of glider flights. What went wrong? Were the wings the wrong size or shape? Did he make a mistake trying to control the direction? Had he tried different designs? Lilienthal had planned on eventually adding a motor to his glider. Who would lead the effort to build a powered flying machine now that Lilienthal was gone? Stories about other men attempting to fly gliders and even powered machines were also showing up in newspapers around this time. It had been big news when the Smithsonian Institution's own Samuel Pierpont Langley (see page 92) flew a model flying machine powered by a small steam engine over the Potomac River—an event made specially newsworthy because the one and only Alexander Graham Bell

OTTO LILIENTHAL
(1848–1896)

Otto Lilienthal spent many boyhood hours watching storks near the Baltic Sea. Seeing these huge white birds flying through the air with ease convinced young Otto that a birdlike wing could be made to carry humans into the sky. Lilienthal became a successful engineer and he would eventually obtain 20 patents for his mining, aviation, and other inventions. Through his experiments in the 1870s, Lilienthal discovered that a curved wing, like that of a bird, glides better. His findings became the book *Birdflight as the Basis for Aviation*. This 1889 book would be studied by all future glider builders—including the Wright brothers.

In 1891 Lilienthal started putting his theories and ideas into practice. He began building more than a dozen different kinds of gliders. Some had a single wing shaped like the outstretched wings of a bat. Other Lilienthal gliders were double-decked biplanes with two sets of wings that looked like giant kites. Most were constructed of flexible strips of willow wood covered with waxed cotton fabric.

Lilienthal in action was quite a sight to behold! He lashed himself into a harness attached to the glider and leaped off of high hills with his legs dangling. Lilienthal and his glider would soar a few hundred feet and then settle to the ground. It was all over within less than a minute. Lilienthal's glider flights thrilled European audiences in the 1890s and news of his feats (along with early photographs) spread across the Atlantic to America. Fans called him the Flying Man.

Lilienthal was able to steer his gliders through shifting his weight. It was controlled piloted flight—something earlier glider flyers couldn't do. Between 1891 and 1896 Lilienthal flew his gliders nearly 2,000 times. Unfortunately, his method of glider control wasn't foolproof. On August 9, 1896, a strong gust hit Lilienthal as he was flying a single-wing glider. The glider's nose tilted up in an instant and the glider stalled. The Flying Man and his glider fell 50 feet (15 m) and crashed to the ground. When rescuers reached him he uttered, "Sacrifices must be made." The crash had broken Lilienthal's spine. He died the next day in a Berlin hospital.

Otto Lilienthal in one of his biplane gliders in 1895.

had photographed it. The efforts of the great engineer Octave Chanute to test gliders that summer had also made news. The brothers wondered and debated as they built bikes: Would one of these men succeed? Or would it be someone else, someone now completely unknown?

Bird Envy

Wilbur and Orville Wright weren't alone—nor were they the first—to dream, wonder, and debate about how humans could take flight. The earliest humans were born into a world already full of flyers. The world's first people undoubtedly watched with envy when birds, bees, and bats magically lifted themselves into the air. Written evidence of humanity's fascination with flying dates back many thousands of years. The ancient Greek myth of Daedalus and his son Icarus tells how the pair escaped from a prison by flying up into the air on wings they'd made of feathers and wax. But Icarus ignores his father's warning and flies too close to the sun. The wax holding his wings together melts and Icarus falls to his death. Medieval "birdmen" who covered themselves in feathers and jumped from towers often met the same fate as Icarus. An 11th-century monk named Eilmer was lucky only to break his

legs after strapping wings onto his hands and feet and gliding from the Wiltshire Abbey tower in England.

These earliest stories and attempts at human flight had something in common. They tried to copy the flight of animals, particularly birds. The Wright brothers also turned to the study of bird flight after Lilienthal's death reignited their interest in flight. A search in the Dayton public library

This statue illustrating the myth of Daedalus and Icarus is in the entryway of the United States Air Force Museum.

Watch the Birds

Since before recorded history, watching birds has inspired people to wonder how we could join them in flight. Nearly every early pioneer of human flight—from Leonardo da Vinci to the Wright brothers—marveled at how our feathered friends made flying look so easy. A number of those early pioneers, including Sir George Cayley and Otto Lilienthal, spent many hours making detailed observations about how birds fly. Their studies helped to solve the mystery of how a wing lifts a bird into the air, and how wings could carry a person into the sky as well. Do some bird watching yourself—who knows what you'll discover!

You'll Need
Notebook
Pen or pencil
Watch with second hand or stopwatch
   (optional)
Bird guidebook (optional)
Binoculars (optional)

1. Find a place to watch birds flying. This can be anywhere. Some good places might be a window near a birdbath or feeder, a city park full of pigeons, a nature preserve, or a lake or pond with ducks. You can often see hawks and vultures soaring while riding in a car on the highway, too.

2. Make a log page in your notebook. Write down the date, time, your location, and the weather (sunny, cloudy, windy).

3. On the log page note the bird you see. Try to identify the bird if you can, or just write a description of it (e.g. "a brown bird the size of a sparrow with a red head").

4. Record how it flies. How does it take off? How does it land? Does it flap its wings all the time, mostly soar, or flap some and soar some? You can use a watch or stopwatch to time how long a bird soars or how many flaps it makes per minute.

5. After watching a number of different birds, think about what you saw. Do all birds fly in the same way? Do large birds fly differently than small birds? Do hawks fly differently than ducks? Does the weather affect bird flight? How?

People have watched birds, like this ring-billed gull, in flight for thousands of years and wondered if they too could somehow fly.

turned up some books on the study of birds (ornithology) and bird flight, which they read carefully. The brothers also observed birds flying in nature and paid attention to how these successful flyers handled high winds and changed speed and direction. "We could not understand that there was anything about a bird that could not be built on a larger scale and used by man," Orville would later say. When they watched birds soar high in the air without even flapping, Orville and Wilbur thought: "If a bird's wing holds it up in the air, so should a wing be able to hold up a person."

Another person who liked to watch birds and dreamed of flying was the Italian artist and inventor Leonardo da Vinci. He was perhaps the first person to envision machines made for carrying a person into the air—what hundreds of years later would be called an airplane. Around 1500 da Vinci sketched and drew plans for a number of flying machines. Some of the designs had wings that rotated like a propeller while others featured flapping wings or gliding wings. As far as anyone knows, the famous Italian artist, scientist, and inventor didn't actually build or fly any of his designs. It's unlikely any of them would have gotten off the ground even if he had. But da Vinci was one of the first thinkers in history to consider human flight simply a technological problem yet to be solved. The common belief of da Vinci's day was, "If God had meant for man to fly, He'd have given him wings."

Heavier or Lighter than Air?

It wouldn't be wings, or any sort of imitation of animal flight, that eventually carried the first humans into the sky. The first person to fly would do so in a machine very different from anything da Vinci sketched, Lilienthal built, or the Wright brothers eventually invented. Bird wings, gliders, helicopter toys, and airplanes are all things that weigh more than the air around them. The fact that an airplane is a heavier-than-air object may be obvious. But the first person in the world to fly did so in a machine that actually weighed less than the air around it—a hot-air balloon.

Hot air rises because it weighs less than colder air. When air heats up, the molecules in the air begin to move faster and faster. Those fast-moving heated air molecules bump into each other and spread out, making a cup full of warm air less dense (lighter) than a cup of cool air. Think about

Flip and Fly Book

Birds may make flying look easy, but bird flight is actually very complicated! A bird in flight is constantly making hundreds of small adjustments to precisely position its wings. A bird changes how far its wings are spread out, the position of the wing tips, and the angle of the wings into the wind. A fun way to slow down bird flight and get a better look is by putting together a flip book.

You'll Need
10–20 index cards
Pen or pencil
Stapler

1. Use the pictures shown on this page to help you draw the steps in bird flight on separate index cards. (You can also photocopy these pictures, cut them out, and paste them onto the cards.)
2. Stack the cards in order so that the top square is the first step.
3. Staple the cards into a book.
4. Make the pages of the book flip by using your thumb. Watch the bird fly!

a   b   c

d   e   f

what happens when you open the door to a hot oven. Whoosh! A blast of hot air quickly rises up out of the oven toward you. Cold air, on the other hand, sinks because it's heavier. A hot-air balloon harnesses this scientific principle and puts it to work lifting people up into the air.

In the 1780s two French papermaking brothers noticed how scraps of paper drifted upward from the flames in their fireplace. Joseph and Étienne Montgolfier (see page 26) began experimenting with trapping heated air in paper sacks. They soon built a large balloon made of linen and lined with paper that they filled with hot air from a fire in the attached balloon basket. It rose. On November 21, 1783, Jean F. Pilatre de Rozier and the Marquis d'Arlandes lifted off in a Montgolfier balloon up into the Paris sky. They flew to a height of around 3,000 feet (900 m) for 25 minutes and landed five miles from where they started. It was the first human free flight in history. Balloon mania soon hit Europe and the sport of ballooning was born. Designs quickly improved and lighter-than-air hydrogen gas replaced heated air. Balloons were soon used for more than just sport. They became the first wartime air vehicles. They were used to check up on the enemy and for communication during the French Revolution, the American Civil War, and the Franco-Prussian War.

Ballooning had been around for more than 100 years, but it didn't interest Wilbur and Orville much. Lighter-than-air flying machines such as balloons seemed like a dead end to them. Ballooning was more like floating than the precision flight of birds. Balloon pilots could only go wherever the wind carried them. Airships would become more controllable with time, as today's blimps prove. But many people working on the problem of human flight (including the Wright brothers) believed that lighter-than-air flying machines weren't the answer. They kept looking to winged creatures for inspiration in solving the mystery of controlled, sustained, heavier-than-air flight.

Flight's Four Forces

Many engineers and enthusiasts attempting to copy bird flight during the 18th and 19th centuries

Hot-air ballooning is still a popular sport and a fun way to fly.

built mechanical bird-wing machines, or ornithopters. These wacky-looking machines were meant to fly, as birds did, using wings that flapped up and down. The newspaper reports of the latest odd-looking ornithopter and its eccentric creator made entertaining reading for invention-watchers like Wilbur and Orville. Readers would be told of wild-looking mechanical contraptions that flapped and sometimes hopped—but never flew.

It was Sir George Cayley (see page 34) who figured out the problem with ornithopters. He did so by first very carefully studying birds and then doing experiments with homemade wings. It just so happens that in the process Cayley also discovered the very principles behind all flight and created a basic airplane design. That's why Sir George Cayley is called the Father of Aerial Navigation. Wilbur and Orville would later study and learn invaluable lessons from Cayley's pioneering work on flight.

What Cayley figured out was how a wing works. Think of a wing's shape in cross-section. (It doesn't matter if it's a bird wing or an airplane wing—they're the same.) That shape is called an airfoil. The Wright brothers would spend years tinkering and perfecting airfoil shapes in the wings they built. The front of the airfoil is a curved hump shape. When the wing moves through the air, it looks like the diagram on page 29. The black lines show how the air moves around the airfoil shape of the wing.

Air may be invisible and seem difficult to feel. But in fact air is all around us, takes up space,

THE MONTGOLFIER BROTHERS

(1740–1810)

More than 100 years before Wilbur and Orville Wright there were two French brothers who made a different kind of flying history. Their names were Joseph Montgolfier (1740–1810) and Étienne Montgolfier (1745–1799).

The Montgolfier brothers were papermakers by profession, but they were also scientists. They were trained in chemistry, physics, and architecture. They ran the family's paper company and developed many new techniques for manufacturing paper that changed the industry. After noticing that scraps of stray paper tended to float upward from a burning fire, Joseph and Étienne started experimenting. The brothers wondered if the burning fire released some special kind of gas. But what was actually happening was that as the air heated up, it became less dense. Heated (less dense) air weighs less, so it rises upward.

The Montgolfier brothers wanted to see if this fact could somehow be put to use carrying a person into the sky. They first went to work building small silk balloons. The small hot-air-filled balloons rose off the ground. By 1783 they were ready to test their hot-air balloons on a grander scale. In June they launched a balloon that was 309 feet (94 m) in diameter, made of linen and paper. The air inside it was heated from a fire on the ground below the balloon's open bottom. The balloon stayed aloft for ten minutes and rose up to 6,000 feet (1,800 m). Three months later, the brothers launched a balloon with animal passengers from the palace grounds at Versailles as King Louis XVI watched. The passengers (a duck, a sheep, and a rooster) survived the eight-minute, two-mile (3.2 km) balloon flight. A month later a human passenger, the scientist Jean F. Pilatre de Rozier, climbed into a much larger Montgolfier balloon. The balloon was anchored with ropes, but it did rise off the ground. On November 21, 1783, Pilatre de Rozier was joined by a French nobleman, the Marquis d'Arlandes, in the large balloon. They ascended to a height of 3,000 feet (900 m) over Paris, stayed aloft for 25 minutes, and traveled five miles. It was the world's first human free flight.

Fly a Balloon

People were flying hot-air and hydrogen-filled balloons 100 years before Bishop Wright gave Wilbur and Orville the flying bat toy. Explore the lighter-than-air technology of ballooning by launching a plastic bag as a hot-air balloon.

You'll Need
Plastic grocery bag
Thin clear tape
Scissors
Rubber band
Hairdryer with a low/warm setting

1. Make sure the grocery bag doesn't have any holes in it. Check it by blowing it up with air first.

2. Stick the end of the hairdryer into the bag's opening. Gather the bag around the end of the hairdryer and wrap a rubber band around it to hold it in place. (An extra pair of hands helps here!)

3. Slide the plastic bag down a bit by pushing down on the rubber band, so that it's around a wider part of the hairdryer. Make sure the rubber band goes all the way around the bag below its handles.

4. Use tape to make a collar around the bag, just above where the rubber band is. Then remove the rubber band and take the bag off the hairdryer.

5. Cut off the handles and top of the bag just above the tape collar. Blow into the bag to make sure your balloon is airtight. If not, try again.

6. Plug in the hairdryer and hold it so the air will blow upward. Slip the bag over the end of the hairdryer.

7. Use one hand to hold the bag's tape collar firmly to the end of the hairdryer and your other hand to hold the hairdryer in position. Switch the hairdryer onto the lowest warm setting.

8. Once the bag is filled with warm hair, do this at the same instant: switch off the hairdryer and release the bag. Watch it rise up!

As young men, the Wright brothers liked to watch birds and picnic at an area called Pinnacle Hill near Dayton. The area was named for rock formations, like this one, called pinnacles. That's Wilbur on the right, in the background.

and weighs a great deal. The air inside an average-size living room weighs about 100 pounds! The weight of air pushing down on Earth is called air pressure. In 1738 Daniel Bernoulli discovered that when air speeds up, its pressure drops. Bernoulli's Principle basically says that fast-moving air has less pressure than slower moving air.

Now go back to the airfoil diagram. Note that the front of the airfoil is higher than the back—it goes downhill. Because of this shape, the air sliding down over the top of the wing speeds up as it goes. Bernoulli's Principle says that faster air has less pressure, so the air zooming over the top of the wing drops in pressure. The higher-pressure air below the airfoil now pushes up on the wing, creating lift. Most of a wing's lift is created by this difference in air pressure. But about

25 percent of a wing's lift comes from air simply striking the bottom of the wing, which pushes that wing upward. You can thank Newton's Third Law of Motion for the extra boost. This natural law says that for every action there is an equal and opposite reaction. The action of the air hitting the bottom of the wing and being bounced downward (the fat arrow in the airfoil diagram) causes an upward push as a reaction.

Lift is the force that pulls an airplane off the ground. Unfortunately, gravity acting on the mass (or weight) of the airplane pulls it back down. That's why kites are made of lightweight materials and why birds have hollow bones. It's also why the Wright brothers would later choose lightweight wood and cloth when building their flying machines. The less weight there was, the weaker the force of gravity, and the more lift was possible.

A wing can only create lift if it's moving through the air. The force that pushes a bird or an airplane forward through the air is called thrust. An airplane's propeller gives it thrust as do the flapping wings of a bird. When you throw a paper airplane your arm muscles provide thrust. So why doesn't that paper airplane fly forever and why couldn't Otto Lilienthal make endless glides? The reason is the fourth force of flight, called drag. Drag is caused by air friction and it works against thrust, slowing down the airplane or bird. Airplanes have a streamlined shape to reduce drag and maximize thrust. Flying—for a bird or a pilot—is a balancing act between these four competing forces of flight: gravity, lift, thrust, and drag.

HOW AN AIRFOIL WORKS

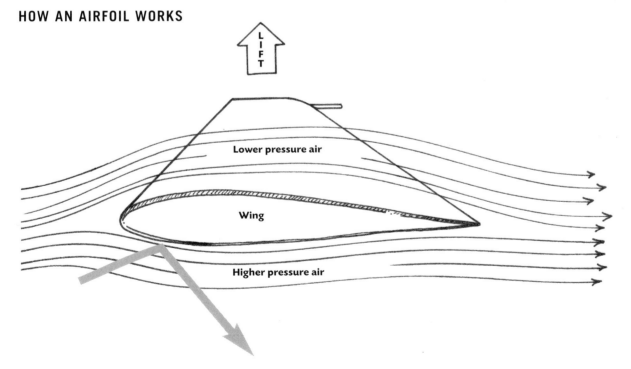

LIFT

Lower pressure air

Wing

Higher pressure air

FLIGHT'S FOUR FORCES

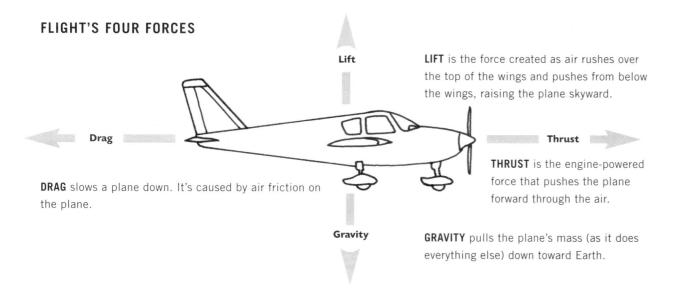

Lift

LIFT is the force created as air rushes over the top of the wings and pushes from below the wings, raising the plane skyward.

Drag

Thrust

THRUST is the engine-powered force that pushes the plane forward through the air.

DRAG slows a plane down. It's caused by air friction on the plane.

Gravity

GRAVITY pulls the plane's mass (as it does everything else) down toward Earth.

Cayley's Contribution

As Sir George Cayley uncovered the four forces of flight—lift, gravity, thrust, and drag—he figured out why ornithopters wouldn't work. A bird gets both thrust and lift from its wings. But like the lesson Orville and Wilbur learned when they tried to make bigger versions of their helicopter toy, Cayley realized that humans could never get enough thrust out of flapping mechanical wings to overcome gravity and drag to produce lift. He decided that an unmoving wing, a fixed wing, could provide lift. But thrust would need to come from elsewhere—perhaps from an engine. After Cayley's historic "On Aerial Navigation" articles were published in 1809 and 1810, most inventors abandoned ornithopter ideas. Inventors, including the Wright brothers, instead concentrated on fixed-winged gliders (both powered and unpowered).

Sir George Cayley also went to work building glider models and then full-size gliders based on the ideas he pioneered. In 1853 Cayley's became the first fixed-wing glider to fly successfully. He also mapped out the basic shape a working powered flying machine needed to have: long fixed wings, a central fuselage, a tail for controlling direction, and a lightweight engine. There were no such engines in Cayley's day and he died 46 years before the first airplane flew. But that first airplane would have all the parts of Cayley's basic design and without his groundwork, the Wright brothers could never have built it.

Wing It!

A wing has a special airfoil shape. An airfoil "foils" the pulling-down force of gravity by creating the upward force of flight—lift. Build your own airfoil and then find the best way to fly it.

You'll Need
Index card or postcard
Tape
Hole punch or sharp pencil
Scissors
Plastic drinking straw
2 bamboo skewers or 2 large metal paper clips
   unbent
Base that the skewers can stick into (chunk of
   Styrofoam, corrugated cardboard, or even
   a large potato)
Hairdryer

1. Fold the card in half. Tape the top half of the card down to the bottom half of the card so that about ¼ inch (6 mm) of the bottom shows. This is an airfoil shape.
2. Use the hole punch (or a sharp pencil) to put two sets of holes in the thickest part of the airfoil.
3. Cut the straw so you get two pieces 2 inches (5 cm) long. Fit these mini-straws through the holes in the airfoil.

4. Set the airfoil on the base and slip a skewer or unbent paper clip through each of the mini-straws and into the base.
5. Use the hairdryer to move air over the airfoil and create lift. Try it both ways—with the flat side of the airfoil on the bottom and on the top. In which position does the airfoil best climb the skewers?

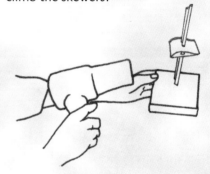

The Letter

By 1899 Wilbur and Orville had read all the information they could find in Dayton about flight. But they needed to know more if they were going to seriously study the subject. How could they find out what others had accomplished so far? The brothers knew that the Smithsonian Institution in Washington, D.C., was interested in heavier-than-air flight. The fact that the secretary of the Smithsonian, Samuel Pierpont Langley, had a $50,000 grant from the U.S. Army to build a flying machine had been in all the newspapers. The Smithsonian seemed like the place to ask for the most up-to-date information. So

Wilbur sat down on May 30th, 1899, and wrote this letter.

Dear Sirs:

I have been interested in the problem of mechanical and human flight ever since as a boy I constructed a number of bats of various sizes after the style of Cayley's and Penaud's machines. My observations since have only convinced me more firmly that human flight is possible and practicable. It is only a question

of knowledge and skill just as in all acrobatic feats. Birds are the most perfectly trained gymnasts in the world and are specially well fitted for their work, and it may be that man will never equal them, but no one who has watched a bird chasing an insect or another bird can doubt that feats are performed which require three or four times the effort required in ordinary flight. I believe that simple flight at

Portrait of Sir George Cayley on display at the United States Air Force Museum.

ACTIVITY

Lift vs. Gravity

Lift is the force that allows an airplane (or bird) to overcome the opposing force of gravity and fly. You can see for yourself how lift and gravity battle it out by watching what happens to a piece of paper as you spin.

You'll Need
Sheet of paper
Enough room to spin

1. Hold the sheet of paper in between your two hands horizontally. Hold your arms out straight.
2. Angle your hands and paper so your thumbs are pointing a little bit toward the ceiling.
3. Start to spin in the direction your thumbs are pointing.
4. After you're spinning, drop your bottom hand. The paper doesn't fall because lift is holding it up. What happens if you stop spinning?

Thrust vs. Drag

Thrust is the force that gives a bird (or airplane) forward motion and gets air moving over a wing. But air constantly rubbing against the surface of the wing causes air resistance, or drag. Drag is the force that slows a flyer down. You can see for yourself how thrust and drag battle it out by watching what happens to a magazine as you spin.

You'll Need
Magazine
Enough room to spin

1. Hold the magazine in between your two hands vertically, so your thumbs point up toward the ceiling. Hold your arms out straight.
2. Start to spin to your left. Spinning provides thrust and gets the magazine (and you!) moving.
3. After you're spinning, drop your left hand. The magazine doesn't fall because drag (or air resistance) is holding it to your hand. What happens if you stop spinning? Could you spin faster (provide more thrust) without the magazine?

least is possible to man and that the experiments and investigations of a large number of independent workers will result in the accumulation of information and knowledge and skill which will finally lead to accomplished flight.

The works on the subject to which I have and access are Marey's and Jamieson's books published by Appleton's and various magazines and cyclopaedic articles. I am about to begin a systematic study of the subject in preparation for practical work to which I expect to devote what time I can spare from my regular business. I wish to obtain such papers as the Smithsonian Institution has published on this subject, and if possible a list of other works in print in the English language. I am an enthusiast, but not a crank in the sense that I have

SIR GEORGE CAYLEY

(1773–1857)

Sir George Cayley was born in Yorkshire, England, three years before the American colonies declared independence. Cayley, a baronet, was a remarkable man whose inventions included caterpillar tracks for vehicles, the hot-air engine, and the tension-spoke wheel. Cayley's discoveries and experiments with flight, however, were his greatest achievements and his passion. He fell in love with flying as a boy when the ballooning craze swept across Europe. But Cayley soon came to believe that winged machines, not balloons, were the future of human flight.

He began studying flight as a young man by experimenting with a Chinese flying top (see page 4). Cayley soon built an improved version that could rise as high as 90 feet (27 m) into the air. Like so many before (and after) him, he next turned his interest to studying birds and how they flew. But Cayley went about his bird watching very scientifically. He studied the shape of bird wings and he weighed, measured, and recorded the speed of different birds in flight. In 1804 he attached a homemade wing to one end of an arm that rotated on a tripod and put weights on the other end of the arm. By using this whirling-arm apparatus, Cayley was able to measure how much weight a wing could lift up as it moved through the air at different speeds and at different angles.

By first carefully studying bird flight and then testing wing angles and shapes, Cayley was able to determine the basic principles of flight. In 1799, to commemorate his discovery, he engraved both sides of a silver disk. On one side was a drawing of an airplane with fixed wings, a tail, and a pilot. On the other side was a diagram illustrating the forces of lift and drag on a wing. George Cayley also put his important ideas to work. In 1853 Cayley's coachman became the first adult in the world to complete a flight in a fixed-wing glider. Legend says that after landing safely in the craft built by 80-year-old Cayley, the terrified coachman immediately quit his job. Through his carefully recorded observations, experiments, and glider trials Cayley invented the science of flight (aeronautics). He defined the principles behind flight and showed how a wing works. He also created the basic design of a modern airplane: a machine with a fixed wing to provide lift, a separate power source for thrust, and a tail for control. These accomplishments secured him a place in history as the Father of Aerial Navigation.

Cayley's 1849 Glider

Wilbur (left) and Orville Wright as young men in 1897.

some pet theories as to the proper construction of a flying machine. I wish to avail myself of all that is already known and then if possible add my mite to help on the future workers who will attain final success. I do not know the terms on which you send out your publications but if you will inform me of the cost I will remit the price.

Yours truly,

Wilbur Wright

Langley's assistant Richard Rathbun politely answered Wilbur's letter and sent a handful of reprinted articles and a reading list to Wilbur Wright of the Wright Cycle Company. He'd filled a lot of requests for information lately. It seems that news of Langley's lucrative grant had brought out of the woodwork all sorts of crackpots who thought themselves inventors. At least Mr. Wright hadn't asked about how to get money to work on his ideas. Little did the assistant know that his packet of information started a process that would not only overshadow his boss's work, but would change the world. Within a few months of receiving the information from the Smithsonian, the Wright brothers would build their first glider.

THREE

Getting Flight Under Control

W hen a packet arrived from the Smithsonian Institution, Wilbur and Orville excitedly opened it. They'd answered Wilbur's letter so quickly! Inside was a letter from Samuel Pierpont Langley's own assistant, Mr. Rathbun. He recommended a number of books to help the brothers get caught up on what was going on in the field of aeronautics, including Langley's *Experiments in Aerodynamics* and Octave Chanute's *Progress in Flying Machines*. The Smithsonian sent a number of reprinted articles along with the letter, including Langley's "Story of Experiments in Mechanical Flight," Louis-Pierre Mouillard's "Empire of the Air," Otto Lilienthal's "The Problem of Flying and Practical Experiments in Soaring," and E. C. Huffaker's "On Soaring Flight." The brothers immediately ordered the recommended books and set to work studying what they'd been sent.

Wilbur and Orville were thrilled to have their hands on some real information. And they were surprised to find out that so many respectable scientists had tackled the problem of human flight. It wasn't just crazy birdmen jumping off buildings and crackpot inventors throwing together goofy-looking ornithopters that were trying to open the sky to humans. "Contrary to our previous impression, we found that men of the very highest standing in the profession of science and invention had attempted to solve the problem," Wilbur later explained. "Among them were such men as Leonardo da Vinci, the greatest universal genius the world has ever known; Sir George Cayley, one of the first men to suggest the idea of the explosion motor; Professor Langley, secretary and head of the Smithsonian Institution; Dr. Bell, inventor of the telephone; Sir Hiram Maxim, inventor of the automatic gun;

← A group of Dayton men in 1900, including the Wright brothers. Wilbur is in the back, the only man without a mustache. Orville is to the right of Wilbur, wearing a lighter-colored jacket.

Mr. O. Chanute, the past president of the American Society of Civil Engineers; Mr. Chas. Parsons, the inventor of the steam turbine; Mr. Thomas A. Edison, Herr Lilienthal, Mr. Ader, Mr. Phillips, and a host of others."

"But one by one, they had been compelled to confess themselves beaten, and had discontinued their efforts," Wilbur later wrote. "In studying their failures we found many points of interest to us." By studying the methods, experiences, and failures of the past few decades Wilbur and Orville were able to get themselves up to speed on what had so far been done to solve the problem of heavier-than-air human flight. The brothers had no desire to repeat past mistakes or waste time fixing what already worked. As Wilbur's letter to the Smithsonian had said, they believed that the problem of human flight would be solved through an accumulation of knowledge and they wanted to add their part to it. But unfortunately not all the information was accurate and the brothers couldn't accept everything they read as the absolute truth. "Those who tried to study the science of aerodynamics knew not what to believe," Wilbur wrote of those early days. "Things which seemed reasonable were very often found to be untrue, and things which seemed unreasonable were sometimes true."

Katharine (right) and her visiting college friend Harriet Silliman in 1899.

Getting Up to Speed

That summer of 1899, Orville and Wilbur would pore over the books and articles discussing every sentence on every page. They thought and talked about little else, which greatly irritated their sister Katharine. She had brought a friend, Harriet Silliman, home with her from Oberlin College to spend their summer break together. But Katharine's brothers were too caught up in their new books about flying machines to properly entertain their sister and Harriet. After carefully studying the information they'd been sent, the brothers realized that those experimenters that had most recently worked on human flight fell (often literally!) into two main groups.

First were those who experimented with powered flight—flying machines with motors and propellers. Lots of money had been spent by famous men in this group of experimenters, but it hadn't bought much success. The rich American inventor of the machine gun, Hiram Maxim, had built a gigantic 7,000-pound (3,200-kg) machine with two steam engines, 100-foot (30-meter) wings, and two propellers in England. Its single flight in 1894 took the iron-wheeled craft only inches into the air before it crashed into a guardrail. The French engineer, Clément Ader, spent $100,000 of his government's money trying to get his steam-powered bat-like contraption more than a few inches off the ground. The French government cut off his funding in 1897.

Samuel Pierpont Langley had successfully flown a propeller-driven aircraft powered by a little steam engine in 1896. Though his flying machine was only a 30-pound (13.6-kg) model, it was enough to convince the U.S. Army to give Langley $50,000 to develop a full-scale version that could carry a person. Wilbur and Orville remembered what had happened when they'd tried to make bigger and bigger versions of their childhood flying helicopter toy. The brothers suspected that Langley's model was also a dead end. It seemed to the Wright brothers that these men were so focused on getting the power needed to lift their machines into the air that they'd overlooked something very important. How were these machines going to be balanced and steered once in the air? None of them had developed ways to control their machines once in flight. Maxim's machine had gone out of control and crashed when it was barely off the ground. Langley believed that with enough thrust, a flying machine would have all the control it needed to overcome any sort of wind or air currents. That didn't make sense to Wilbur.

The second group of experimenters was those who worked on unpowered gliding. While Sir George Cayley had flown a couple of gliders, they'd really just been one-time flyers. They couldn't be flown again and again. Repetition is important to science and engineering. Just because something works or happens one time doesn't make it a scientific fact. For it to be scientifically true (and a practical design) it must work again and again. But in the past decade, three people had built dependable gliders that could make repeatable flights of 100 feet (30 m) or more lasting 10 seconds or so. In Europe there was the famous German Flying Man Otto Lilienthal (see page 20) and the Scotsman Perry Pilcher. In America, the engineer Octave Chanute's (see page 52) gliding success on the dunes of Indiana in 1896 had made the newspapers.

Wilbur and Orville thought that this second group of men were on the right track. The problems of flight needed to be worked out first with gliders—power beyond the wind could be added later. Not to mention that the brothers had no hope of being able to fund the construction of expensive powered flying machines that would likely crash. But while Wilbur and Orville sided with the gliding men in their approach, they believed that Lilienthal, Pilcher, and Chanute were also overlooking the importance of controlling their flying machines just as Maxim and Langley were. Lilienthal's weight-shifting control method had failed to prevent his own death, after all. And his follower, Perry Pilcher, would also die in a crash of an uncontrollable glider in 1899. Chanute's team had its share of mishaps as well while gliding— Chanute insisted on having a doctor nearby in case of a crash.

Wilbur and Orville spent the summer discussing and debating the failures and successes of Maxim and Ader, Lilienthal and Langley, Pilcher and Chanute. Unlike most flying enthusiasts of the time, they didn't just grab a hammer and start throwing together some crazy contraption they hoped would finally be the first machine to fly.

Incredible as it may seem, the Wright brothers were really the first ones to look at the problem of human flight in a scientific way. First they did their homework, researching what everyone else had done up till then. Then they decided to think through the basics and work out the fundamentals of flight. The brothers asked each other: "What exactly is needed to fly?" Wilbur would later spell out their answer in a lecture to engineers, saying, "The difficulties which obstruct the pathway to success in flying-machine construction are of three general classes: (1) those which relate to the construction of the sustaining wings; (2) those which relate to the generation and application of the power required to drive the machine through the air; (3) those which relate to the balancing and steering of the machine after it is actually in flight."

The brothers had boiled down the problem of flight to three things: wings, power, and control. Now Wilbur and Orville asked themselves the next question: Which of these three are solved problems and which still need to be worked out? Wings were a done deal, Wilbur concluded. Cayley had figured out how a wing produces lift decades ago. Lilienthal's books clearly spelled out the proper curved shape needed for glider wings. And hadn't the gliding men proven these ideas when they lifted into the air and soared? Next was the problem of the power needed to give a flying machine enough thrust. This too was a problem well in hand, thought the brothers. Langley's model proved that spinning propellers could power a flying machine through the air. Yes, the steam

THREE WAYS TO MOVE

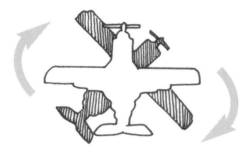

YAW is an airplane's right and left movement.

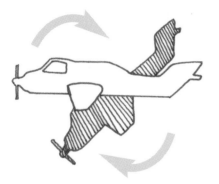

PITCH is an airplane's climbing and diving movement.

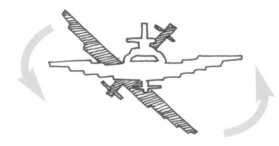

ROLL is an airplane's tilting or banking movement.

engines that turned Langley's propellers would be too heavy when scaled up for a person-size aircraft. But Orville knew firsthand from working on his friend Cordy Ruse's early automobile that gasoline-powered engines were the way of the future. These small engines were getting lighter and better all the time.

The third fundamental needed for flight, control, was another matter. It was a problem yet to be solved. "This inability to balance and steer still confronts the students of the flying problem," Wilbur would confess to the engineers at his lecture. "When this one feature has been worked out, the age of flying machines will have arrived, for all other difficulties are of minor importance." After only a couple of months of reading and talking, the brothers had boiled down humanity's enduring quest for flight to a single problem: how to control an airplane once it was in the air.

Controlling Flight

Up until the Wright brothers' day, inventors working on flying machines had mostly concentrated on one thing—getting up into the air. No one worried much about steering the flying craft one way or another. It was hard enough just getting the contraptions off the ground! Many believed that once the flying part was worked out, maneuvering could come later. But Orville and Wilbur disagreed. The Wright brothers saw controlling the

aircraft as a fundamental part of successful flight. They believed that throwing an unstable wobbly aircraft up into the air was a waste of time. What good was getting up in the air if you immediately spun out of control? Anyone who's ever made a paper airplane that dives straight to the ground would agree. The Wright brothers were convinced that human flight couldn't be done without dependable ways to keep the aircraft stable and maneuverable. Besides being harder to fly, an unstable and uncontrollable flying machine was too dangerous. Lilienthal's fatal accident was still fresh in the brothers' memories.

Some experimenters had tried to make more stable flying machines and gliders by using flexible tails and wings or by shifting their weight. But to test an idea about how to control a flying machine, you first had to be able to fly it and survive. Wilbur and Orville would soon have plenty of bumps, bruises, and black eyes to prove the fact that experimenting with flight control wasn't easy research. Another reason control during flight had remained a mystery was that moving around in the air was a brand-new experience for humans. There was a lot about how air moved, flowed, gusted, and blew that no one understood back then. The airplane would be the very first vehicle that needed to be controlled in air's three different dimensions. An airplane moves in three directions; it has three axes of motion. An airplane moves right and left, it moves up and down as it climbs and dives, and it moves side to side as it tilts and balances. These three directions are called yaw, pitch, and roll.

The easiest of the directions to understand is steering right or left, called yaw. A driver steers a car right or left by moving the steering wheel in the direction the wheels should go. A boat is turned right or left with a rudder. Swing a rudder to the left and the water flowing past pushes the rudder to the right, making the boat turn left. Air is like water in many ways as it flows in currents. So most experimenters, including the Wright brothers, reasoned that a kind of air rudder would work for a flying machine, too.

But unlike a car or boat, an airplane also climbs and dives in the air. This up and down direction is called pitch. Primitive submarines had been used in the American Civil War and they had pitch control to climb and dive in the water. Wilbur and Orville understood that pitch is really just like yaw—only turned on its side. A vertical rudder controls yaw and moves a boat or submarine left and right. A horizontal rudder can in the same way control pitch and moves a submarine up and down in the water. A horizontal rudder is called an elevator. An elevator controls an airplane's up and down movement, just as a building elevator takes passengers up and down.

The third direction of movement, roll, was the one that flight experimenters were having trouble with. Many inventors didn't even realize it existed. The fact that a flying machine moves right and left (yaw) and has to climb and dive (pitch) is pretty obvious. But an airplane also tilts from side to side, which is called roll. The Wright brothers would be among the first to realize that an airplane's wingtips have to balance to fly

straight, and tilt to bank turns. Think of a small airplane taxiing on the ground. When it makes a right turn (yaw) onto a runway the nose of the airplane moves right, but the wings stay in the same position. However, that same airplane turns very differently in the air. Imagine you're in the airplane as it makes a tight turn to the right in flight. You feel the turn in the same way you do in a car turning—you're pushed against the side of your seat. But the airplane also tips up on the left side at the same time. The passengers sitting on the left side of the airplane are higher during the turn. This tilting or banking movement is roll. Birds use roll too when turning. Just think of a hawk soaring. As it turns right it doesn't just turn its body to the right. Its wings tilt up so the left wing is higher while it banks the turn.

Why did Wilbur and Orville understand roll when other flight experimenters did not? Believe it or not, it was because they rode bicycles. A bike moves right and left (yaw) but it also tips over (roll)! When steering a bike, you don't just turn the handlebars, you also lean into the turn. This leaning movement is the same as banking or rolling an airplane. Riding bicycles taught the Wright brothers other lessons about flying, too. It taught them that some vehicles are more stable when they're moving. A bike is totally unstable when it's not moving, after all. And isn't a bike much harder to steer and balance when you're moving very slowly? A stopped bike won't even stand up without a kickstand. But once it's moving forward, an experienced rider is easily balanced—the bike becomes stable. The brothers

This turkey vulture is banking a turn. Its lower wing dropped after the bird pulled in the feathers on that wingtip, reducing that wing's lift just like in wing warping.

Pitch, Roll, and Yaw

An airplane has three axes of motion. It moves in three different directions, called pitch, yaw, and roll. An airplane moves right and left (yaw), it moves up and down as it climbs and dives (pitch), and it moves side to side as it tilts and balances (roll). Not until the Wright brothers were able to control all three directions of movement in their glider were they able to successfully fly. By building a model of an airplane and its three axes, you can see these three directions for yourself.

You'll Need
Rectangular foam piece
Lightweight cardboard (poster board, cereal box, or file folder)
3 bamboo skewers
Scissors
Pencil
Tape or glue

1. Build a model of an airplane. Use the foam for the fuselage. Cut wings, a tail rudder, and a tail elevator out of lightweight cardboard. You can give them all movable control flaps by pressing down hard while drawing a line with a pencil. Attach the wings and tail sections to the fuselage with tape or glue, or just cut slits into the foam and slip them in. Don't worry if your model doesn't look perfect! It doesn't need to fly for this activity.

2. Stick one of the skewers straight down through the fuselage behind the wings. Twist the skewer in between your fingers, making the airplane move right and left. This is **yaw.** It's controlled by the rudder.

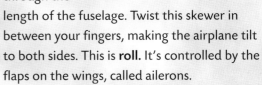

3. Stick another of the skewers straight down through the side of the fuselage behind the wings. Twist this skewer in between your fingers, making the airplane move up and down. This is **pitch.** It's controlled by the elevator.

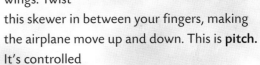

4. Carefully stick the last skewer straight down through the length of the fuselage. Twist this skewer in between your fingers, making the airplane tilt to both sides. This is **roll.** It's controlled by the flaps on the wings, called ailerons.

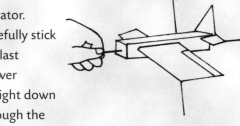

thought that controlling a glider or flying machine was just like riding a bike. It was a skill you could learn by practicing.

After reducing the mystery of human flight to solving the problem of balancing and steering a glider, the Wright brothers decided that they wanted to take on the challenge. Orville and Wilbur weren't the types to leave figuring something out to others. They were raised to think through problems for themselves and to believe in their own ideas. With Lilienthal and Pilcher dead, Langley very likely on the wrong track, and Chanute no longer experimenting, the field of human flight looked wide open. Wilbur believed they could contribute to the field through experimenting with gliders. He saw it as his chance to finally do something important with his life and make his mark. Orville seemed more enchanted by the thought of soaring on the wind. What great sport gliding would be!

Bicyclists lean during turns to remain stable.

Modern airplanes use wing flaps, or ailerons, like those on the left to control roll. The tail on the right has both a vertical striped rudder and horizontal flaps for an elevator.

Warping Wings

Wilbur and Orville wanted to build a better glider. There had to be a better way to control it than by swinging your legs back and forth to shift weight. But what would be a better way to control a glider in gusts of wind and shifting air currents? Some of the glider builders on Chanute's team thought it was to make rudders and wings that automatically bent or flapped to and fro in the wind. That way the glider would give a little in the wind and not be felled by a powerful gust. The Wright brothers thought the idea of building gliders that could be passively stable was ridiculous and unworkable. Wilbur believed that

a pilot should be able to control all three directions of movement, including roll. A flying machine's pilot shouldn't just ride out the bumps and hope for the best. The pilot should expertly operate control over the machine, argued Wilbur. The brothers reasoned that Lilienthal was right to try to control his glider. Weight shifting just wasn't a particularly good way to do it. What would be a better way to balance a glider?

Like so many before them, the Wright brothers once again turned to their feathered friends for inspiration. A soaring bird doesn't maneuver by shifting its weight, as Lilienthal tried to do, observed Wilbur. It instead balances itself and turns by changing how it angles its wings into the moving air. The amount of lift a wing creates varies depending on its angle into the wind, called the angle of attack. As the front edge of a wing tilts upward, the curved part of the wing becomes a steeper slope. The steeper the wing's slope, the faster the air slides down the top of the wing, and the more lift is created.

Wilbur observed that birds are able to balance themselves through wind gusts and also bank through turns by changing the position of their wings. When banking during a turn, a bird angles the forward edge of one outstretched wing up and the other wing down. There's now more lift on the wing with a steeper angle, and this wing tilts and rises up while the other wing tilts down. The bird rolls through the turn and then levels out as it changes the angles of its wings again. "Here was the silent birth of all that underlies human flight," noted Wilbur after watching soaring buzzards. But how could the Wrights change the angle and shape of a glider's wings?

If a pilot could vary the angle of attack of the glider's wingtips, Orville thought it should work just as it did for the birds. He quickly sketched out a wing with adjustable wingtips controlled by levers and cogs. But it just wasn't a practical design for those days. Separating the wingtips from the rest of the wing would make the wood and canvas wings too weak. (Orville's idea was, however, very like the wing flaps, or ailerons, used to control roll on airplanes today.) They needed a way to adjust the angles of the wings and still keep them as one strong rigid piece.

The answer came to Wilbur one day in July 1899. He was tending the bike shop by himself as Orville and his sister were out showing Harriet Silliman around Dayton. A customer had stopped in to buy an inner tube for a bicycle tire. Wilbur opened the long narrow cardboard box it came in and handed the customer the inner tube. As they chatted, Wilbur absentmindedly held the box in both hands. Without thinking, he began twisting the box by its ends in opposite directions, as if he were wringing out a dishcloth. Even though he was twisting the ends of a flimsy box in opposite directions, it didn't tear. Then it hit Wilbur. The long narrow box was like the wings of a double-decked biplane glider! Twisting, or warping, flexible wings in the same way as he was twisting the box would cause one wingtip to go up and the other down. This change in shape would make a glider tilt and bank just like a soaring bird. Wilbur realized that this warping of wings could be used to control roll in a glider and in flying machines.

Kites Aren't Just for Kids

Wilbur tore off the ends of the inner tube box so that the twisting was easier to see on the rectangular cardboard tube. He took the box home with him that night and showed Orville what he'd discovered. After talking about it, the brothers were so sure that wing warping, as they called it, would work that they quit looking for any other methods to control roll. Instead they set about building an experimental glider that they planned to fly and control with cords, like a big kite.

The experimental glider kite was a biplane, with double wings stacked on top of each other. Wilbur and Orville made this first of their experimental aircraft in the bicycle shop's workroom. Its wings were 5 feet (1.5 m) long and 13 inches (33 cm) wide and were covered with shellacked cloth. This made them airtight. Strips of wood and wires connected the double wings and a small elevator was attached to the front. Cords were attached to the glider kite's four wingtips. The two cords from the right-side wings were attached to one stick and the two left-side cords were attached to another stick. The Wrights planned to fly—and control—the kite by holding onto a stick in each hand.

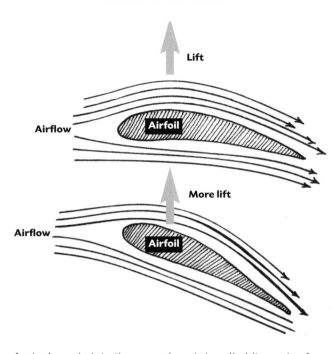

ANGLE OF ATTACK

A wing's angle into the oncoming air is called its angle of attack. The steeper the angle, the faster the air slides down the wing, and the more lift is created.

While Orville was on a camping trip with Katharine and some of her friends, Wilbur decided to try to fly the glider kite. The 32-year-old bicycle maker took the kite out to a field where he and his brother and their friends had flown kites as boys. The kite handled beautifully. By pulling on the cords' stick handles, Wilbur made the kite climb, dive, and—most importantly—roll to the right or left. The wing warping worked! Just as expected, the upturned wing rose up and the downturned wing dipped down. The glider kite swooped and dove just like a hawk.

The sight of a grown man in a suit and tie flying a giant double-decker kite soon drew a crowd of curious kids. Wilbur put on quite a show for them. He even once made the kite dive so quickly and steeply that the young onlookers had to throw themselves to the ground to avoid being hit. Wilbur and Orville were excited about the glider kite's performance—wing warping worked! The brothers had built the world's first flying craft that had both controlled roll and pitch. Wilbur and Orville knew that they were onto something. They decided it was time to take the next step. The Wright brothers immediately began working on a full-scale pilot-carrying glider.

One of the Wrights' summer camping trips to Shoup's Mill, Ohio.

Doing the Math

The Wright brothers knew that turning their design for a kite into one for a piloted glider wouldn't be easy. There was so much to figure out! How would the pilot control the wing warping and elevator? The 5-foot (1.5-m) kite design was obviously too small, but just how big did a glider need to be to carry a person? What should the wingspan be, or the wing's length from tip to tip? And what should the wing's width, or chord, be? And what about the wing's airfoil curve, called the camber? Should it have a steep camber with a perfect half-moon

Glide a Glider

Before building a full-scale glider, the Wright brothers first made model gliders to try out their ideas. You can make—and fly—your own model glider by following these instructions.

You'll Need
12-inch (30-cm) long square wood rod
Foam or lightweight cardboard plates
Glue
Newspaper
Scissors
Sharpened pencil
Ruler
Tape
Pennies
Stapler

1. You can use either foam or cardboard plates for the wings and tail sections. Cut out two 7½-inch by 2½-inch (19-cm by 6-cm) rectangles for the wings. Cut out one 5-inch by 2½-inch (13-cm by 6-cm) rectangle for the elevator.

2. Use a sharpened pencil and a ruler to make ailerons on the wing rectangles. Start from one end and draw the line about an inch parallel to the edge, as shown. Stop once you've gone 5 inches (13 cm) from the end. Press down hard enough to score the foam or cardboard. Cut a short slit from the edge to the end of the line. You should now have a bendable flap. Make an aileron on the other wing rectangle, too.

3. Use a sharpened pencil and a ruler to make a wing flap on the elevator. Start from one end and draw the line about an inch parallel to the edge along the long side.

4. To make a rudder, first cut out a 4-inch by 2½-inch (10-cm by 6-cm) rectangle. Use a sharpened pencil and a ruler to make a wing flap on the right end of the rudder. Start from the top and draw the line about an inch parallel to the right edge along a short side.

5. Draw another line that connects the bottom left-hand corner of the rectangle to the point 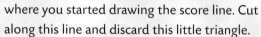 where you started drawing the score line. Cut along this line and discard this little triangle.

6. Cut out a shallow notch on the bottom of the rudder, as shown. This notch is to fit the rudder over the elevator, so its thickness depends on how thick your elevator is.

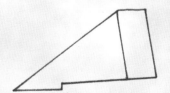

7. Put down some newspaper. Set the elevator onto the end of the wood rod so that the flap completely hangs over the end of the rod. Unfold a stapler and staple the elevator onto the rod. Then glue it from the bottom.

8. Line up the wings so that their top edge is about 2 inches (5 cm) from the rod's end. Glue them onto the rod. Prop up each wing with a book so that they dry with a slight V angle. Once they're dry, you can also glue the wings from the bottom for extra support or add some tape.

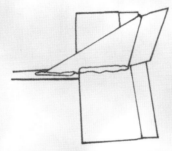

9. Glue the rudder onto the rod and elevator, as shown. If you're having trouble getting the rudder to stay up while drying, some strips of tape will give it some support.

10. Once the glue is dry, it's ready to fly! Find an open area. Hold onto the glider's middle rod and gently toss it forward into the air. Your glider may need some weight on its nose or along the rod, depending on what you made

the wings out of. Just tape on pennies. You can experiment to find out how many pennies your glider needs (and where) to fly best. Move the rudder, ailerons, and elevator to control your glider. Can you make it fly straight? Fly right or left?

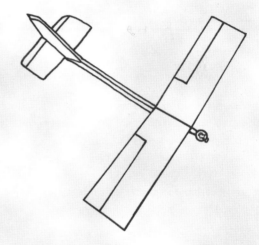

A GLIDER'S PARTS AND MEASURES

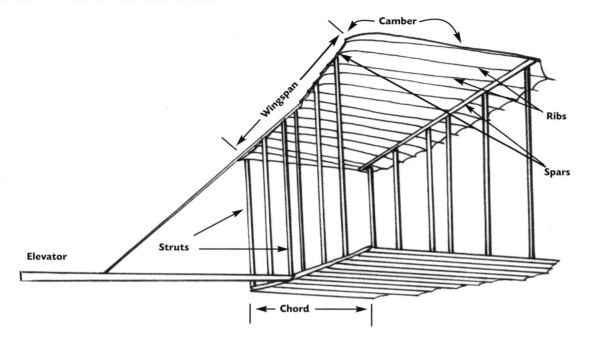

The wingspan is the tip-to-tip length of the wings, and the chord is the front-to-rear width. The camber is the amount of curvature or steepness of slope the wing has. The framework of the glider wings was made of long wooden spars that ran the length of the wings and many ribs that ran from spar to spar. Wood support struts connected the two stacked wings and were trussed with wire for added support.

shape, or should it be steeper at the front and shallower at the back?

The Wright brothers turned to Otto Lilienthal and Octave Chanute's books and papers for answers. Both Lilienthal and Chanute had used formulas or equations in their work. These formulas calculated how many pounds of lift a wing created based on the following things: the wing's size (wingspan and chord) and weight; the wind speed; the air pressure; and something called the lift coefficient. Lift coefficient is a measure of how well an airfoil produces lift—think of it as the measurable strength of an airfoil. Every different shape of airfoil at every different angle of attack creates a particular amount of lift, so it has its own lift coefficient. Airfoils with different cambers have

different lift coefficients. And two identical airfoils that have different angles of attack will have two different lift coefficients. Lilienthal had published tables of lift-coefficient numbers for different airfoil shapes and attack angles. They were known as Lilienthal's lift tables and were what everyone (including Chanute) used to calculate the lift of their glider wings. Like any equation, as long as you know everything in the equation except one thing, you can use the other parts to calculate the one remaining unknown.

After putting what they knew and Lilienthal's numbers into the formulas and doing the math, this is what the brothers calculated: To build a glider made of wood and cloth that would lift up its own weight and that of a 140-pound (63-kg) man, the glider would need 20-foot-long (6 m) wings and steady winds of about 15 miles per hour (24 kph). That's pretty windy, which ruled out Dayton as a testing ground. Dayton just wasn't windy enough. Wilbur wrote the Weather Bureau in Washington around Thanksgiving of 1899. He asked for information about how strong the winds were around Chicago. Wilbur knew that Octave Chanute had done his glider experiments near there. Maybe the winds would be strong and steady enough there for the Wrights' experiments as well. The Weather Bureau's chief wrote back to Wilbur, sending along not only Chicago wind speeds but also the September wind speeds taken at 120 Weather Bureau stations all over the country.

Orville and Wilbur studied the tables of wind speeds when they had time during the winter of

Engineer, aviation historian, and glider experimenter Octave Chanute.

1900. But they were very busy building bikes for the upcoming spring and summer season. The brothers decided that whatever glider testing they hoped to do would have to be in the fall when the bike business was slow. Chicago would be too cold at that time of year. They needed someplace farther south, but not too far from Dayton. In the spring Wilbur made an important decision. He decided to write the great engineer Octave Chanute himself and ask him where a good place would be to test a glider in September or October. Wilbur wasn't sure he'd get an answer. Octave Chanute was an important man, after all. But it never hurts to try.

Seeking Advice and Finding a Friend

When Octave Chanute opened Wilbur's letter he found five handwritten pages on the blue stationery of the Wright Cycle Company. The letter, dated May 13, 1900, began quite oddly, sounding a bit like the confessions of an obsessed man. "Dear Sir," wrote Wilbur. "For some years I have been afflicted with the belief that flight is possible to man. My disease has increased in severity and I feel that it will soon cost me an increased amount of money if not my life...."

Luckily, the bicycle maker went on to explain that he was hoping to "devote my entire time for a few months to experiment in this field" and that he agreed with Chanute's belief that gliding

had to be mastered before propellers and motors could be added successfully. Wilbur told Chanute that he believed that Lilienthal failed because his 10-second flights didn't allow him enough time to really practice flying, and because Lilienthal's control method of shifting his weight was flawed. Wilbur even hinted to Chanute about the brothers' wing-warping discovery, writing "My observation of the flight of buzzards leads me to believe that they regain their lateral balance [roll], when partly overturned by a gust of wind, by a torsion [twisting] of the tips of the wings."

Wilbur outlined his plans in the letter, including the rather wacky idea of suspending a glider from "a light tower about one hundred and fifty feet high" with a rope and pulley. Wilbur wrote that this would "enable me to remain in the air for practice by the hour instead of by the second." Toward the end of the long letter, Wilbur finally got around to asking the engineer for advice: "My business requires that my experimental work be confined to the months between September and January and I would be particularly thankful for advice as to a suitable locality where I could depend on winds of about fifteen miles per hour without rain or too inclement weather."

Chanute was a man who'd made his fame and fortune through railroad construction, bridge building, and other engineering feats. But the dream of human flight was his true passion. He was happy to get a letter from a fellow flying enthusiast, and this unknown bicycle company owner impressed him. Chanute wrote back to Wilbur, inviting him to meet with him any time

OCTAVE CHANUTE

(1832–1910)

Octave Chanute was born in Paris and moved to the United States with his family as a child. He became a famous civil engineer, building railroads, bridges, stockyards, and utility systems for towns. He supervised the construction of the first bridge to span the Missouri River in Kansas City just after the end of the American Civil War. The town of Chanute, Kansas, in the southeast part of the state, was named in his honor.

It was during a vacation to Europe in 1875 that Chanute picked up his interest in human flight. He read about the work of English engineers such as Sir George Cayley and recognized a true engineering challenge when he saw one. He began to study aeronautics. Chanute corresponded with Otto Lilienthal and other gliding men and flying-machine experimenters over many years and then wrote *Progress in Flying Machines.* Chanute's important book is a complete history of humanity's attempts at flight up until 1894. This book was on the recommended reading list the Wright brothers received from the Smithsonian. After publishing his book, Chanute began to design gliders of his own. He thought that wings of gliders could be trussed together for support, just like the bridges he'd built. Chanute's glider designs had as many as six tiers of stacked wings! But his double-decked biplane design tested on the dunes of Indiana in 1896 was the best glider of its day—and the one the Wright brothers would improve upon.

Perhaps as important as his own work was the support Chanute gave the Wright brothers. Wilbur's letter to Chanute, written in May 1900 started 10 years of correspondence based on the shared dream of human flight. After Chanute's death, Wilbur wrote, "If he had not lived, the entire history of progress in flying would have been other than it has been."

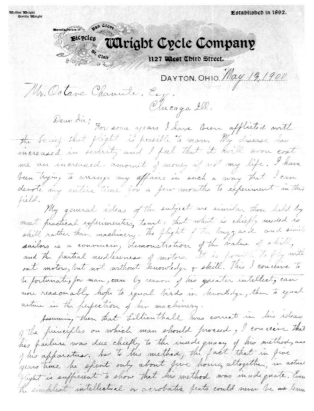

Wilbur Wright's letter to Octave Chanute written on May 13, 1900.

he was in Chicago. He encouraged Wilbur to keep him up to date on his progress. Chanute politely warned Wilbur that his idea of hanging a glider from a tower could lead to "accidents from rotation of apparatus or collision with supports." Chanute said that he preferred "preliminary learning on a sand hill" and recommended that the Wrights find some nice soft sand dunes to glide on. "The two most suitable locations for winter experiments which I know of are near San Diego, California, and St. James City (Pine Island), Florida, on account of the steady sea breezes which I have found to blow there. These, however, are deficient in sand hills, and perhaps even better locations can be found on the Atlantic coasts of South Carolina or Georgia."

Orville and Wilbur were happy to hear back from the famous engineer and appreciated his recommendations. But California and Florida were way too far from Dayton. They'd spend half the time they had available just getting there! The nearer Atlantic coast seemed a better bet. The brothers returned to the information sent by the Weather Bureau and Wilbur noticed that the winds at a place called Kitty Hawk, North Carolina, averaged 10 to 20 miles an hour (16 to 32 kph). It was a remote fishing village on the Outer Banks, an area of endless sandy beaches. It sounded

The beach at Kitty Hawk

perfect. Wilbur wrote the Weather Bureau office at Kitty Hawk and got a reply. Joseph J. Dosher, the only employee at the tiny Kitty Hawk weather station, wrote back saying, "The beach here is about one mile wide and clear of trees." Dosher reported that the autumn winds blew from the north and northeast, but warned that while there was food in the town, there were no hotels or boarding houses. "You will have to bring tents."

FOUR

Gliding at Kitty Hawk

Orville and Wilbur decided that they'd head down to Kitty Hawk as soon as the bicycle business slowed down in the fall. Wilbur wrote Chanute of their plans, saying in a letter dated August 10, 1900, "It is my intention to begin shortly the construction of a full-size glider." The brothers quickly started work on their first glider in Dayton. But it wouldn't be completely assembled until they reached Kitty Hawk. Train travel was the only sensible way to get anywhere so far away in those days, and the glider would have to be crated and shipped in pieces. The brothers figured there was no sense in putting it completely together when they'd just have to take it apart to crate it up anyway.

The bicycle workroom was turned into a wood shop as Wilbur cut and shaped the pieces of the glider's frame and struts. He cut pieces of ash into ribs for the glider's wings, and bent the ribs into a curved shape with steam. The brothers bought and crated up metal fasteners, tools, and the steel wire used to truss the wings together. They cut and sewed yards of white French sateen cotton fabric on Katharine's sewing machine to cover the wings. Long sleeves were sewn into the wing fabric so that the 18-foot (5.5-m) spars could be slipped in from the sides later. The glider materials cost a total of $15. Wilbur and Orville packed up everything they thought they'd need—and might not be able to buy—in remote Kitty Hawk. But Wilbur was having trouble finding wood for the long wing spars. The local lumberyard didn't have the 18-foot pieces of spruce Wilbur wanted. Chanute suggested that Wilbur look in Cincinnati, Ohio. But Wilbur instead planned to buy cut spars in Norfolk, Virginia, a large city en route to Kitty Hawk. He'd later be sorry that he hadn't tried Cincinnati.

← Wilbur gliding down Big Kill Devil Hill in October of 1902.

Design a Paper Glider

Did you know that paper airplanes are really gliders? They are! Some paper airplane shapes are better at long glides, while others are better at hitting targets. Still others are great for doing tricks, like flying loops. You can build a basic paper glider design, experiment with it, and then perfect it.

You'll Need
8½-inch by 11-inch (22-cm by 28-cm) sheets
    of paper
Scissors
Paper clips
Tape measure
Notebook
Pencil or pen

1. Make a basic paper plane prototype with a sheet of paper. First fold the sheet of paper in half lengthwise, crease well, and reopen. Next, turn in one top edge of the paper and line it up with the center crease. Crease well. Repeat this process for the other side.

2. Bring each of the folded edges to the center crease line and fold. Crease well. Fold the glider in half along the center crease. Crease well again.

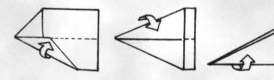

3. Now decide what you want your paper glider to do: fly very far, be able to hit a target, or make a loop. The rest is up to you! Think about what kind of wing shape will make this happen. Then decide how far to bend down the wings—a lot or a little. You can also add weight to the glider's nose or tail by adding paper clips. How will you angle the wings?

4. Test your paper glider. Use the tape measure to record the distance flown or the distance from the target. Keep track of your designs and their performance in your notebook.

By the time August turned to September, Wilbur was nearly ready to go. "We are in an uproar getting Will off," Katharine wrote her father who was away as usual on church business. "If they can arrange it, Orv will go down as soon as Will gets the [glider] machine ready." Wilbur also wrote his father, telling him that he was heading for Kitty Hawk to do "some experiments with a flying machine. It is my belief that flight is possible and, while I am taking up the investigation for pleasure rather than profit, I think there is a slight possibility of achieving fame and fortune from it.... At any rate, I shall have an outing of several weeks and see a part of the world I have never before visited."

Can't Get There from Here?

It's about 660 miles (1,060 km) from Dayton, Ohio, to Kitty Hawk, North Carolina. It takes 13 hours to drive that distance by car today. But traveling those same 660 miles at the turn of the last century was quite a journey. Wilbur boarded the 6:30 evening train in Dayton on the evening of Thursday, September 5, 1900. Twenty-four hours later, he got off the train in Point Comfort, Virginia. Friday evening he got himself and all his crates onto a ferry that crossed the mouth of Chesapeake Bay and docked at Norfolk, Virginia. After a night in a hotel, Wilbur spent a humid, scorching, 100-degree (38°C) Saturday looking for spruce

spars. No luck. Wilbur finally gave up and bought the only option available in all of Norfolk—16-foot (4.9-m) pine spars. The original 18-foot (5.5 m) wing design should have flown in winds of 12 miles per hour (19 kph), the brothers calculated. Shorter wings would create less lift. Now they'd need winds of 15 miles per hour (24 kph).

Wilbur loaded up his gear, including the pine spars, and left Norfolk on a train headed for swampy Elizabeth City, North Carolina. He spent the Sunday evening after his arrival on the docks, trying to figure out how to get himself, the crated glider, and all the other gear to Kitty Hawk. There were no roads or bridges connecting the Outer Banks to the mainland in 1900. Wilbur needed to find someone to take him and all his crates the 35 miles (56 km) by boat. It wasn't easy. "No one seemed to know anything about the place, or how to get there," Wilbur later recalled. Finally, on Tuesday, a man agreed to haul Wilbur and his cargo on his fishing schooner. A small skiff took Wilbur and the cargo out to the anchored schooner, and Wilbur wasn't happy with what he found. "The sails were rotten, the ropes badly worn and the rudder post half rotted off, and the cabin so dirty and vermin-infested that I kept out of it from first to last," Wilbur recalled. The 35-mile trip took two long days in the sailboat. They sprang a leak during a storm and had to stop and repair the old boat before continuing. During the entire trip Wilbur ate only a jar of jelly that Katharine had tucked into his luggage. He didn't trust the food on board the rat-infested ship.

Wilbur and Orville enjoyed exploring the beach near their camp. They loved to birdwatch and look for sea creatures, like this sand crab.

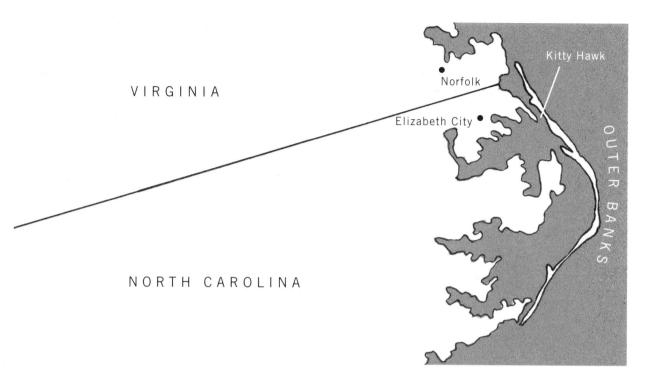

It was late in the evening on Thursday September 12 when Wilbur finally set foot in Kitty Hawk. It had taken an entire week to get there! Fortunately, an exhausted Wilbur was warmly welcomed by local postmaster Bill Tate and his family. The Tate house (with its combined post office) was one of only a handful of fishermen's homes scattered along the entire bay at Kitty Hawk in 1900. Wilbur stayed with the Tates until Orville arrived a week and a half later.

Orville left Dayton after hiring a young man to fill in at the bike shop. The youngest Wright son arrived at Kitty Hawk loaded down with gear, including a tent, gas lamp, and cots. He'd also brought along some things hard to come by in Kitty Hawk—canned food, coffee, tea, and sugar.

The brothers set up camp. They had to carry water by bucket nearly a quarter mile from a well. Remembering how Orville had nearly died of typhoid four years earlier, the brothers wisely boiled the water. They quickly fell into a routine with Orville cooking and Wilbur washing up. The brothers also fell in love with the charm and natural beauty of the Outer Banks. "The sunsets here are the prettiest I have ever seen," Orville wrote his sister back to Dayton. "The clouds light up in all colors in the background, with deep blue clouds of various shapes fringed with gold before." Wilbur would write Octave Chanute later that fall saying what a great place Kitty Hawk was to watch birds. "I think at least a hundred buzzards, eagles, ospreys, and hawks made their

The Tate family on the porch of the Kitty Hawk Post Office and their home. →

The brothers first tested the 1900 glider by flying it as a kite.

← The Wright brothers' lonely 1900 camp near Kitty Hawk.

home within a half mile of our camp." Calm nights were spent with Orville playing his mandolin and Wilbur the harmonica. But some nights the wind blew so hard that it seemed as if the tent would blow away. "We certainly can't complain of the place," Orville wrote Katharine. "We came down here for wind and sand, and we have got them."

Taking the Plunge

Once settled in, Orville and Wilbur went to work putting together the glider. They borrowed Mrs. Tate's sewing machine and used it to alter the wing coverings so they'd fit the shorter pine spars Wilbur had bought in Norfolk. When the wings were completely assembled they had a wingspan of 17 feet (5.2 m) and a 5-foot (1.5-m) chord. The wings were connected with struts and trussed with wire. The wires that warped the wings and controlled roll in the glider ran over pulleys between the two wings. The wing-warping wires attached to a T-bar that the pilot controlled with his feet. The elevator, which controlled pitch (climbing and diving), was attached to the front of the glider. The pilot operated the elevator by raising and lowering its control arms.

When the 1900 glider was fully assembled in early October, it had about 165 square feet (15.3 sq. m) of surface area and weighed about 50 pounds (23 kg). Both Chanute and Lilienthal had flown double-decker biplane gliders, but the

Wrights' glider looked very different. No one had ever put an elevator in the front before—nor made the elevator controllable. No one had ever had wing warping on a glider before either. But the most obvious difference was that the pilot of a Wright glider didn't dangle down like someone hang gliding. The pilot lay facedown on the lower wing. Many experimenters thought this was suicide. The pilot would surely plow face first into the ground! But Wilbur and Orville knew that having a pilot's body hanging down below the glider greatly increased the amount of drag due to air friction. They calculated that lying horizontal on the wing cut the amount of drag in half. The less drag there is, the more thrust is available. That meant they could do more flying in weaker winds (a glider's source of thrust). Going face first was worth it, they decided.

Wilbur knew that Bishop Wright worried about the health and safety of his once-sickly third son. Wilbur wrote his father in late September reporting that "I have my machine nearly finished. It is not to have a motor and is not expected to fly in any true sense of the word. My idea is merely to experiment and practice with a view of solving the problem of equilibrium [balance and steering]." He assured Milton Wright that he'd be careful and that "I do not expect to rise many feet from the ground, and in case I am upset there is nothing but soft sand to strike."

Thoughts of plunging nose first into the "soft" sand were put aside for the time being. The Wright brothers started testing the glider by first flying it with ropes attached, much like a kite. They

Tom Tate was Kitty Hawk postmaster Bill Tate's 10-year-old nephew. He rode on the 1900 glider when the brothers flew it as a kite. The glider is behind Tom and his drum fish.

tested and measured the amount of drag on the glider by attaching a fish-weighing scale to each of the taut ropes holding the glider. Winds were carefully measured with a handheld anemometer that Joe Dosher, the Weather Bureau employee, had loaned the Wright brothers. They tested the glider's lift with different weights by adding heavy chains or Bill Tate's 70-pound (32-kg) nephew Tom. Could the smaller-than-planned wings lift a 140-pound (64-kg) pilot? It seemed that it might, though the amount of lift they were measuring seemed much less than they should be getting according to their calculations. The wings weren't creating as much lift as Lilienthal's lift tables predicted they should.

Another stumbling block was the wind. Kitty Hawk was so windy that sometimes the men couldn't sleep from all the flapping noise of their tent. In October Orville wrote to Katharine that they'd been unable to fly the glider the past two days because they'd had winds of 36 miles per hour (58 kph). The following "morning the Kitty Hawkers were out early peering around the edge of the woods and out of their upstairs windows to see whether our camp was still in existence." The brothers, called Mr. Wright by total strangers wherever they went, had caused quite a stir in the tiny town. Maybe it was because they claimed to be building a flying machine. Or perhaps it was due to the fact that anyone walking by their camp reported hearing loud arguing at all times of the day and night. Perhaps these brothers were considered odd city folk because, despite the fact that they were camping on the beach each night,

they came out of their tent each morning dressed like bankers—wool suits, starched collars, and neckties!

While sometimes it was too windy, other days were too calm to fly the glider. Orville and Wilbur realized that the wind speeds on the tables from the Weather Bureau that sounded so perfect for glider testing were actually averaged speeds for the entire month. They weren't the everyday wind speed. The brothers had to wait around for days until the winds were just right to test their glider. Wild wind gusts were also common. A few days into their testing, a gust of wind caught an edge of the glider and tossed it 20 feet (6 m). The brothers talked about giving up and going home as they dragged the crumpled pieces back to camp. What was the use? But the damage looked repairable the next morning after a good night's sleep. It took three days of hard work to fix the glider and get back to testing it. After three weeks of experimenting with the glider as a kite, Orville and Wilbur decided to try flying it with a pilot. How else would they know if their glider could fly? Besides, time was running out—it was now or never. It'd been six weeks since Wilbur left Dayton, and a recent telegram from Katharine said there were problems at the bicycle shop. The brothers promised to be home by the end of the October.

A few days later the winds were finally the right speed. A rented horse and wagon hauled the glider four miles down the beach to some high sand dunes called Kill Devil Hills. Orville, Wilbur, and their faithful friend Bill Tate then lugged the

The Wright brothers' view of Kitty Hawk Bay from their 1900 camp.

glider 100 feet (30 m) up the tallest dune, called Big Hill. Once on top of the hill, Wilbur lay down on the glider's bottom wing. He grasped an elevator control arm in each hand so he'd be ready to direct the glider's nose downward when he wanted to land. His feet rested on both sides of the T-bar that controlled the wing warping, though for now it was tied off. Orville and Bill Tate each grabbed an end of a wing and started running downhill into the wind. If a wingtip threatened to twist up a bit, Bill Tate or Orville pressed it down, manually warping the wings as they trotted down the hill. Quickly the air speeding over the shining white wings began pulling the glider upward.

The 1900 glider was wrecked by a gust of wind. It took Orville and Wilbur three days to repair it and get back to their experiments.

The best of those lasted 15 to 20 seconds and went a good 300 to 400 feet (90 to 120 m). This was as good, if not better, than Lilienthal's glides. The brothers were also very impressed with how the pitch control worked with the movable front elevator. They'd left a gap in the bottom wing so that the pilot could drop his legs down to the ground at the last second to help land the glider without dragging it on the sand too much. But the pitch control worked well, and the glider went from speeds of up to 30 miles per hour (48 kph) to land softly with the pilot still lying down. The brothers decided to try controlling the wing warping, too. So they tried the last few glides with the pilot working the wing warping with the T-bar foot control. Doing both proved somewhat tricky. But unlike any other glider flyers before them, the Wright brothers were truly operating a flying machine with real controls. What a day!

It turned out to be the only day for free flight gliding that year. The winds died down the next day and didn't pick up again. The brothers were out of time. They abandoned the glider to the Tates, and Mrs. Tate salvaged its sateen cloth. After giving it a good scrubbing, she cut and sewed the cloth into dresses for her two young daughters. Wilbur and Orville headed back to Dayton, their conversation filled with ideas and plans for building a better glider. "We were very much pleased with the general results of the trip," Wilbur later summed up. "For setting out as we did, with almost revolutionary theories on many points, and an entirely untried form of machine,

Big Hill, the tallest dune at Kill Devil Hills, where the Wright brothers glided.

Orville and Bill Tate could feel the glider getting lighter and lighter. It gradually pulled away from their grasp and glided ahead of the men. It was flying on its own! Lying on the wing, Wilbur smiled through the blowing sand and salty wind. He was flying! Then, as if he'd been doing it all his life, Wilbur moved the elevator to point the glider downward and landed it.

It was the first of about a dozen free glider flights that Wilbur made on October 20, 1900.

we considered it quite a point to be able to return without having our pet theories completely knocked in the head by the hard logic of experience, and our own brains dashed out in the bargain." He assured Chanute in a letter that the "experiments will be continued along the same line next year."

Back to Dayton, Back to Work

Wilbur and Orville fell back into their old routine soon after arriving home from their exciting time in North Carolina. The brothers went back to work at the cycle shop and spent the fall and

Measure the Wind

The Wright brothers chose Kitty Hawk to test their gliders because of the strong winds. They carefully measured the wind every day using an anemometer. Make this anemometer and measure the wind in your neighborhood.

You'll Need
Large protractor
Ping-Pong ball
Tape
12 inches (30 cm) of strong thread or fishing
    line

1. Tape one end of the thread to the Ping-Pong ball and the other end to the center point on the base of the protractor.
2. Hold your anemometer level, with the base of the protractor up and make sure that the ball swings freely.
3. To measure the wind, stand facing into the wind and hold the anemometer away from your body. The higher the ball is lifted, the stronger the wind. A reading of 85 degrees in angle on the protractor indicates a wind speed of about 6 miles per hour (10 kph). Each additional 5 degrees adds about another 2 mph (3.2 kph).

Wilbur and Orville's brother Lorin with three of his children—Horace, Ivonette, and Leontine.

winter making bicycles for the upcoming busy spring season. Bishop Wright continued his work for the United Brethren Church, still traveling even though he was now a grandfather in his seventies. Though Wilbur and Orville never married or had children of their own, they had a warm extended family life. Their older brother Lorin, his wife Netta, and their four children lived only a block away from the Hawthorn Street home. Everyone spent Sundays and holidays together at Grandpa Wright's house. The three generations would spend the day reading stories, playing

games, and making homemade taffy, caramel, or fudge. Orville and Wilbur would make puppets out of sheet metal and put on shadow puppet shows. Uncle Wilbur and Orville's shop was also a favorite spot for the children. "When my mother had an errand taking her downtown, and had one child she couldn't take with her, we were dropped off at the bicycle shop," recalled Lorin Wright's daughter Ivonette. "Either Orville or Wilbur, or both, baby-sat us. They were never too busy to entertain us."

Life in the Wright home on Hawthorne Street did have some new twists in that first year of the 20th century. Katharine had put her college degree to work teaching Latin and history at a Dayton high school. She still lived at home but no longer had time to keep house for her widowed father and two bachelor brothers. A 14-year-old girl named Carrie Kayler was hired to come in during the day to help cook and clean for the family. The brothers teased Carrie because she was so small for her age that she had to stand on a chair to light the gas lamp in the kitchen. But she became a valued part of the Wright home. She worked for the family for the next 48 years.

While Wilbur and Orville were back into their routine of work and home, flying never left their thoughts—or their conversation. They loudly debated the details of the plans for a new glider as they put together bikes at the shop. Carrie recalled that the brothers would start arguing nearly every evening at home just about the time she was doing the supper dishes. Orville would sit on one side of the living room fireplace in a chair with his arms folded and Wilbur would sit on the other side with his legs stretched out and his hands folded behind his head. They'd argue for a while over some point, then fall silent for a while thinking about each other's comments before diving back into verbal battle.

Upgrading the Glider

The brothers had a lot to debate. While they were thrilled with the fact that their 1900 glider had flown, it had had some problems. The biggest problem was that the 1900 glider's wings hadn't created as much lift as Wilbur and Orville had carefully calculated it should. Why not? They had three ideas. Maybe the fabric covering the wings wasn't airtight enough. The brothers hadn't sealed it with varnish or shellac as they had the kite's cloth, after all. A second possible reason was that the wing's camber, or slope, was too flat. They'd chosen a flatter camber than Lilienthal had, and the brothers also noticed that the wings had flattened out over time. The ash ribs bent into a curved shape with steam seemed to straighten out a bit while they experimented at Kitty Hawk. The third reason that they might not be getting the amount of lift they should was the most worrisome. Wilbur and Orville's calculations had used numbers from Lilienthal's published lift tables. What if the numbers in Lilienthal's tables were wrong?

Wilbur and Orville discussed and argued over the possibilities all winter. Chanute and other flight experimenters accepted Lilienthal's tables as correct, so the brothers decided not to throw them out—for now. They also decided that their basic design was a good one and stuck with it. Wilbur said as much to Octave Chanute in a letter updating the engineer on their progress: "The [new 1901] glider itself will be built on exactly the same general plan as our last year's machine but will be larger and of improved construction in its details." Wilbur and Orville decided to fix the problem of not enough lift by simply making the glider bigger. They got to work building a bigger glider with more steeply curved wings.

The 1901 glider had a 22-foot (6.7-m) wingspan and a 7-foot (2.1-m) chord. That meant it had a surface area of 290 square feet (27 sq. m), as compared to the 1900 glider's 165 square feet (15.3 sq. m). The new glider weighed about 100 pounds (45 kg), twice the weight of previous year's, and was fitted with wooden sled-runner-looking skids to keep the elevator safe during landing. The wing camber would be curved nearly twice as steeply as the 1900 glider's wings. It would be the biggest glider ever flown. A glider this big would have been impossible to fly without the Wright brothers' groundbreaking control systems. They kept the same forward movable elevator in the 1901 glider. But they changed the wing-warping control so that the wires were connected to a hip cradle instead of a T-bar operated by the feet. Now when the pilot lay down

WING WARPING

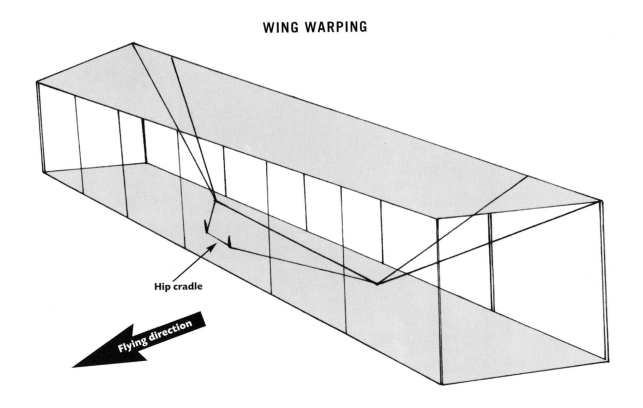

Hip cradle

Flying direction

The 1901 glider's wing warping was operated with a hip cradle. When the pilot shifted his hips right, wires pulled the left wingtips down, brought the right wingtips up, and the glider banked right.

on the bottom wing, his hips slid into a wooden cradle. By shifting his hips one way or the other, the pilot could operate the wing warping.

A Summer Gone South?

A man named Charlie Taylor started working at the Wright Cycle Company in June 1901. He was a talented machinist and someone Wilbur and Orville trusted to run the business—even though he was a cigar smoker known to occasionally swear! With the shop now in good hands, the brothers had more time to work on their new glider. They even decided that they could leave town before the busy bicycle season ended.

Wilbur, Orville, the crated glider, and all their gear left Dayton on a train bound for Norfolk, Virginia, on July 7, 1901. A bad storm held the brothers up for a couple of days once they reached Elizabeth City, North Carolina. The Weather Bureau station at Kitty Hawk had recorded winds during the storm as high as 93 miles per hour (150 kph)—a record! The storm ended a summer drought at Kitty Hawk and was followed by a week of heavy rain. After spending their first night with the Tates, Wilbur and Orville hauled their crates, gear, and a stack of lumber four miles down the beach to Kill Devil Hills. The group of tall sand dunes was where Wilbur had flown the first glider last October. It was to be the new site for their camp. They wanted to be closer to where they'd be flying the bigger (and hopefully better) 1901 glider. But all they did that first day in the pouring rain was set up a tent and crawl inside.

The Wright brothers spent their first week at Kill Devil Hills building a big wooden shed. "The building is a grand institution," Orville proudly wrote home to his sister. "[It has] big doors hinged at the top, which we swing open and prop up." It'd be used as a hangar for the glider and a workshop. The men would keep living in the tent. About the time that the shed was finally done, company showed up. Edward C. Huffaker had worked with Octave Chanute and had authored *On Soaring*

Flight, the pamphlet sent to Wilbur by the Smithsonian. Chanute had written the Wrights earlier that summer to ask if Huffaker and a young doctor named George A. Spratt could come and observe their experiments. Orville and Wilbur were expecting the human guests, but they had no way of foreseeing the insect invaders.

A week of rain following a drought created a giant breeding ground for mosquitoes. Orville described the insect onslaught as "a swarm of mosquitoes which came in a mighty cloud, almost darkening the sun. That was the beginning of the most miserable existence I have ever passed through. The agonies of typhoid fever with its attending starvation are as nothing in comparison. But there was no escape. The sand and grass and trees and hills and everything were crawling with them. They chewed us clear through our underwear and socks. Lumps began swelling up all over my body like hen's eggs." The men tried to escape at night by wrapping themselves in blankets and sleeping under netting. Finally they ended up burning old tree stumps, though they nearly suffocated from the smoke. By the time the mosquitoes were gone the men had the glider put together and were ready to test it. The insects may have moved on, but more problems were on the way.

Trudging up a 100-foot (30-m) hill of sand with a 100-pound (45 kg) glider in tow isn't easy, especially in the heat of an Outer Banks July day. But at least Orville and Wilbur had lots of helpers in 1901. Besides Huffaker and Spratt, there was Bill Tate and his half brother Dan Tate. The men

hauled the finished glider up Big Hill, the tallest dune. As he had the year before, pilot Wilbur lay on the bottom wing while two men grabbed the wingtips and started running down the hill. When he felt the wind taking over and holding up the glider, Wilbur yelled, "Let go!" to the helpers.

The team of sweltering experimenters heaved the giant glider up the hill nine times on the first day before Wilbur had a decent glide. By scooting

The Wright brothers had lots of company at their Kitty Hawk camp in 1901. Seated left to right are Octave Chanute, Orville, and Edward C. Huffaker. Wilbur is standing on the right side inside the newly build shed.

Wilbur just after landing in the 1901 glider at Kill Devil Hills.

First Pests, Now Problems

What in the world was wrong with the new "improved" glider? The pitch was really hard to control with the elevator, something that had worked so well last year! Wilbur was having to lift and drop the elevator a lot more just to keep the glider from running into the ground or soaring up into a stall. Maybe the elevator was too big? The Wright brothers cut the elevator down to nearly half the original size. It didn't help. Wilbur and Orville flew the glider as a kite for a couple of days to test it. The results weren't promising. They were only getting a third of the amount of lift they should be, according to calculations based on Lilienthal's lift tables. The 1900 glider had even gotten more lift than this! Something had to be very wrong with the wings. Was it the new fabric? The 1901 glider was covered in a tightly woven and sturdy white muslin called Pride of the West that was mostly used to make women's undergarments. They hadn't sealed the fabric with varnish or shellac to save on weight. Maybe it wasn't airtight enough? The brothers made two small model wings with the muslin fabric. They coated one with varnish and left the other unsealed. But after testing the model wings, they found no difference in lift. The fabric was fine.

Wilbur and Orville tried to think the problem through. It wasn't the elevator and it wasn't the fabric. What else was different about this year's glider that could be causing the problem? The brothers talked, argued, and decided that it was

himself as far back as he could on the lower wing, Wilbur finally made a glide of 315 feet (96 m) that lasted 19 seconds. While the observers were impressed with the first day of gliding, Orville and Wilbur were not. "Our first experiments were rather disappointing," Orville wrote home. "The machine refused to act like our machine last year and at times seemed to be entirely beyond our control."

the wing camber. The wings of this year's glider had a different shape. They'd made the 1901 glider's wings with a steeper camber, like Lilienthal's wings. The brothers had thought that the flatter camber was the reason why the 1900 glider didn't have the lift it should. But the steeper camber had only made things worse in the 1901 glider. Orville and Wilbur knew they could change the camber back to that of the 1900 glider by retrussing the wings to make them flatter. Thank goodness they'd had the bright idea of making the wings adjustable back in Dayton!

Just about the time that Wilbur and Orville were finished tinkering with the wings, Octave Chanute arrived at camp. It was already August. The elderly engineer was on hand to see if adjusting the camber did the trick. It did, or at least it helped. The ever-growing team of experts first flew the glider as a kite for a couple of days, and then Wilbur got ready to free fly it. He wouldn't let his younger brother pilot the problematic glider. It was too dangerous.

The men trudged up the Big Hill, Wilbur climbed back onto the bottom wing, and they launched the refurbished glider. Going back to the flatter camber had improved it. Wilbur again smiled as he smoothly sailed down the dune, easily controlling the pitch to land. Wilbur made a dozen good glides that day, the best one covering 389 feet (119 m). Chanute was very impressed with the smooth, straight, level glides—and Wilbur's expert piloting. These polite bicycle makers from Ohio had glided farther than anyone else ever had before!

Orville and Wilbur weren't at Kitty Hawk just to break distance records. They were much less impressed with themselves and the rehabbed glider than Chanute was. Yes, it was better. But even with the changes in camber, the glider was still getting nowhere near the amount of lift the brothers had calculated it should. And yes, the 1901 glider was now making nice, smooth, straight glides. But when the brothers tried to turn using the wing-warping controls, the unthinkable was happening. Wilbur was having trouble turning the glider! Wing warping was their biggest discovery so far. Why wasn't it working? By shifting his hips (which pulled on the wing-warping wires) Wilbur made the angle of the right wingtip rise and that of the left wingtip fall. The upturned right wingtip caught more lift and the glider pivoted on the lower left wingtip, banking the glider left. This is how wing warping was supposed to work. But partway through the turn, the lower wing would start to tremble and the glider would reverse the direction of the turn, nearly spinning out of control. Trying to figure out what was going on, Wilbur tried making another turn during the next glide. He had to straighten out quickly and land the glider just to keep from spinning out of control. The wing warping was turning out to be dangerous.

During another glide, Wilbur was flying low over the sand when the glider's left wingtip dipped down. He shifted his hips to the right to correct it, but forgot to also move the elevator up. The glider instantly dove into the sand. The skids buried into the sand and Wilbur slammed forward into the elevator. The elevator was smashed—and so was Wilbur's face. He had a black eye, bruised nose, and cuts on his face. The elevator was fixable. But after repairing it, the brothers only dared to test the problem by flying the glider as a kite. The wing-warping problem happened even then. What was causing this mysterious problem?

Chanute and his colleagues headed back to civilization and left the brothers alone at camp. Rain soon moved in and didn't let up. Orville and Wilbur started packing for home feeling defeated and frustrated. It was the third week of August. What was the use of staying any longer? Their new glider hadn't turned out to be the bigger, better model they'd hoped for. Why were their lift calculations always wrong? And what in the world could be causing this new wing-warping problem?

Orville and Wilbur left Kitty Hawk in late August and headed home to Dayton. Wilbur caught a summer cold on the long, silent train ride. "We doubted that we would ever resume our experiments," wrote Wilbur later. Sure, they'd set a new distance record for gliding. "Yet when we looked at the time and money which we had expended, and considered the progress made and the distance yet to go, we considered our experiments a failure." Wilbur predicted that "men would sometime fly, but that it would not be within our lifetime."

Regaining Confidence

The train from Norfolk finally pulled into the Dayton station. The Wright brothers got off the train and Wilbur headed straight for bed. He was sick with a bad cold and depressed about the experiments at Kill Devil Hills. Everything that had gone wrong kept going through his head over and over. "Those lift calculations were never right!" he thought. "How are we supposed to figure out how to change the wings when the calculations never come out right anyway? And that problem with our wing warping!" Wilbur had wanted to contribute to the pursuit of human flight through the experiments. Now he doubted that he'd ever make much of a difference.

Meanwhile Orville spent Labor Day weekend holed up in a shed in the backyard. Inside the shed the brothers had set up a photography darkroom. Orville carefully developed the glass-plate negatives from the camera they'd taken with them to North Carolina. Orville then printed pictures from the negatives and took them to Wilbur. The pictures weren't images of problems and failure. They showed Wilbur soaring above the sand in a beautiful white-winged glider. Seeing himself in flight helped Wilbur remember all that they had accomplished and how far they'd come. Maybe the problems could be worked out after all.

Octave Chanute also helped lift Wilbur's spirits—by giving him something else to worry about. Chanute invited Wilbur to give a speech at a meeting of the Western Society of Engineers in Chicago. Chanute wanted others to hear about the brothers' gliding experiments and see their photographs. Wilbur wasn't sure about it. He wasn't a professor or an engineer; he hadn't even been to college! The thought of answering technical questions from a large audience of learned men was a bit overwhelming. But Katharine talked him into accepting the invitation and the brothers were soon back to debating the problems of their glider. "We don't hear anything but flying machine...from morning till night," complained Katharine to her father in a letter. "I'll be glad when school begins so I can escape."

Writing the speech helped Wilbur gain some perspective on their accomplishments and think through the summer's problems. By the time he left for Chicago, he was again confident about their abilities. Dressed in Orville's more stylish clothes, Wilbur got over his stage fright and gave an impressive lecture. The lecture put the Wright brothers on the map. It was printed and reprinted in a number of magazines and scientific journals. No one now doubted that these two brothers were serious experimenters making real progress toward building a flying machine.

Speaking in Chicago and talking to the engineers there helped give Wilbur the confidence the brothers needed to make the next giant leap forward. They had to stop trusting the work of their hero, Otto Lilienthal, which everyone else accepted as the absolute truth. The Flying Man's lift tables had to be wrong, the Wrights reasoned. It was the only answer left as to why their calcu-

lations never came out right. "...[W]e saw that the calculations upon which all flying-machines had been based were unreliable, and that all were simply groping in the dark," Wilbur wrote later. "Having set out with absolute faith in the existing scientific data, we were driven to doubt one thing after another, till finally, after two years of experiment, we cast it all aside, and decided to rely entirely upon our own investigations." The

Seeing this photo of himself piloting the 1901 glider helped inspire Wilbur to get back to work.

two high school–educated bicycle makers decided to put Lilienthal's famous lift tables to the test.

Testing the Tables

Wilbur and Orville rigged a horizontal bike wheel (without a tire) onto the front of a bike. They attached some sheet metal flag-like model wings, or airfoils, to the rim of the wheel at very particular angles. Then they rode the bike around to create wind on the little airfoils and watched how they balanced against the moving air. It confirmed their suspicions—the model wings didn't create the amount of lift they should according to Lilienthal's tables. "I am now absolutely certain that Lilienthal's table is very seriously in error," Wilbur wrote Chanute in October 1901. The brothers now knew that they had to throw out those lift tables. But there was no other source of airfoil lift and drag coefficients for them to use in wing calculations. Wilbur and Orville decided to determine the numbers for themselves. They could build and test a number of airfoil shapes at different angles of attack and generate their own tables. Lilienthal had done this using a whirling arm balanced with weights, much like Cayley's original whirling-arm apparatus. Obviously that hadn't worked so well. But what would be better? The brothers decided to build a wind tunnel.

A wind tunnel is a testing lab for studying the effects of flowing air (wind) on an aircraft. Some modern wind tunnels are big enough to fit an entire passenger jet inside and have house-size fans blowing in air. Orville and Wilbur's wind tunnel may have been smaller, but it measured lift and drag nearly as accurately as wind tunnels used today. The brothers built their wind tunnel in a workroom behind the bicycle shop. It was a wooden box about 6 feet (2 m) long and 16 inches (40 cm) wide and deep. They put a glass window into the top so they could see inside and built a fan into one end. The fan ran off an engine that Charlie Taylor had built to power the tools in the shop.

Wilbur and Orville built dozens of model wings, or airfoils, to test inside the wind tunnel. They fashioned the airfoils out of tin, iron, steel, and wax using tools from the bike shop. The brothers made miniature wings in all kinds of shapes and sizes and with different cambers—thick, thin, curved, and flat. Inside the wind tunnel the airfoils were set at a particular angle of attack and the fan turned on. Wilbur and Orville recorded how much the wing moved at that angle with air blowing on it. This told them how much lift the wing created. The Wright brothers now had a way to make their own accurate lift tables.

Wilbur and Orville worked most of the winter testing about 200 different airfoils in the wind tunnel. Like the best scientists they were careful to do each test identically. They kept all the conditions the same, always standing in the same place and never moving any equipment around. Each airfoil was tested at different angles of attack. Orville later wrote, "I believe we possessed

This replica of the Wright brothers' 1901 wind tunnel is on display at the United States Air Force Museum. The inset picture shows the testing apparatus that went inside the wind tunnel. It held the different airfoils and measured the amounts of lift and drag.

more data on cambered surfaces, a hundred times over, than all of our predecessors put together." In fact, they had gathered all the data they'd need to design aircraft for the next 10 years.

Settling In for a Long Stay

Once Wilbur and Orville felt sure about their numbers, they began designing a new glider. They'd finally be able to calculate precisely how much lift the wings could create! The 1902 glider would be the biggest yet. Its wingspan was 32 feet (10 m) with a 5-foot (1.5-m) chord, giving it 305 square feet (28 sq. m) of surface area. The brothers' wind tunnel tests determined that a long narrow wing with a fairly flat camber was the best shape.

Wilbur and Orville had also given a lot of thought to the problem of the wing warping. How could they stop the glider from changing directions and spinning out of control as it banked? They came up with a plan. Help the roll control by adding more yaw control. The 1902 glider would have a rudder to help it also turn horizontally (yaw) when banking (roll) turns. The rudder was made of two unmovable vertical pieces attached to the back of the glider, like a little biplane wing turned on its side.

The Wright brothers kept the hip cradle control for the wing warping and hand control for the elevator that was in the 1902 glider. They also used the same Pride of the West fabric on the

FRANCIS HERBERT WENHAM

(1824–1908)

Francis Wenham was an English scientist who added a number of important pieces to the puzzle of human flight. Wenham was among the first to say that a successful glider should be multiplane, or have more than one wing. In 1858 he tested some mulitplane gliders (like the one below). They didn't fly, but he did discover a lot about how wings worked. In 1866 Wenham read a paper he had written about his tests to a brand-new scientific society, the Royal Aeronautical Society of Great Britain. Octave Chanute, and later the Wright brothers, incorporated many of Wenham's discoveries into their own biplane glider designs.

Wenham continued to study wing shapes. Like most scientists up until then he used a whirling arm balanced with weights to measure the amount of lift and drag on different wing shapes. But Wenham didn't trust the results he was getting. A whirling arm goes around and around, so the wing travels through air it has just stirred up. He correctly believed that this wasn't a very good way to get accurate measurements. So in 1871 he built a device that blew air straight at a model wing. Francis Herbert Wenham invented the most important tool of aerodynamics—the wind tunnel. It was 12 feet (3.7 m) long and 18 inches (46 cm) square in width. A steam engine powered a fan that blew air down the tube. He mounted various model wing shapes in the tunnel, just as Orville and Wilbur would do 30 years later. He was finally able to accurately measure the lift and drag on the model wings created by the air rushing by. Scientists were amazed by the results. Wenham's results showed that wing shapes were actually able to lift up much more weight than anyone had thought. This discovery gave researchers of the day reason to believe that powered human flight was indeed possible.

Testing with Wind

Only after testing hundreds of differently shaped airfoils were the Wright brothers able to design the best wings for their glider. In the Chapter 2 activity "Wing It!" (page 31), you built a wing and discovered how its shape created lift. By using the same setup, you can now test various airfoils to see how differently each performs.

You'll Need
Scrap paper, poster board, cardboard, foam
    meat trays, and aluminum foil
Tape
Plastic drinking straw
Hole punch or sharp pencil
Set-up from "Wing It!" (2 bamboo skewers or
    2 large, metal, unbent paper clips and a
    base that they can stick into, such as a
    chunk of Styrofoam, corrugated cardboard,
    or a large potato)
Hairdryer

1. Build airfoils by following steps 1 through 3 of "Wing It" on page 31. But instead of using a folded postcard, use new materials such as heavier or lighter paper, plastic, or aluminum foil. Consider using foam meat plates or corrugated cardboard and using an unfolded shape. Change the camber of the airfoils or make the leading edge wider or narrower than the back. (Remember that you will need to get two straw pieces through the airfoil.)

2. Test each airfoil. Set it on the base and slip a skewer or unbent paper clip through each of the mini-straws and into the base, as you did in "Wing It!" Then use the hairdryer to move air over the airfoil and create lift. Which airfoil shapes and materials rise up higher and easier? Can you conclude why?

wings, sewing in the pockets for the ribs and spars. Katharine good-naturedly complained to her father in a letter about her brothers' frantic efforts to finish up and head for Kitty Hawk that busy summer. "Will spins the sewing machine around by the hour while Orv squats around marking the places to sew. There is no place in the house to live but I'll be lonesome enough by this time next week and wish that I could have some of their racket around."

Luck was with Wilbur and Orville as they traveled to the Outer Banks late that August. A schooner bound for Kitty Hawk was in the harbor at Elizabeth City when the brothers arrived on the train. Its captain agreed to transport them and all their gear. Dan Tate helped the Wright brothers haul their crates and supplies down to the Kill Devil Hills camp. The men spent a week repairing the wind-battered shed and adding on living space. Wilbur and Orville wouldn't spend any nights listening to the tent flapping in the wind this year!

Wilbur wrote to their 1901 visitor, George Spratt, saying how much better everything at

The "immensely improved" kitchen at the Wright 1902 camp at Kitty Hawk.

camp was this year: "First, we have not seen a dozen mosquitoes in the two weeks and a half we have been here. Second, we fitted up our living arrangements much more comfortably than last year. Our kitchen is immensely improved, and then we have made beds on the second floor and now sleep aloft. It is an improvement over cots." Wilbur also proudly reported to the young doctor that they'd dug a new water well and brought a better bike for riding on sand. "It takes only about an hour to make the round trip to Kitty Hawk instead of three hours as before."

Taking the time to make their camp more comfortable was worth it. It was going to be Wilbur and Orville's longest stay yet and they'd have lots of visitors again.

Getting Back to Gliding

By mid-September the 1902 glider was put together and ready to fly. Orville was especially excited as he'd finally get to pilot the glider! Both brothers took turns gliding down Big Hill after being launched with the help of Dan Tate. The controls took some getting used to and Wilbur and Orville stuck to short glides while they practiced. The steering problem with the wing warping seemed to be fixed now by the new tail rudder. At least it seemed fixed *most* of the time.

"I was sailing along smoothly without any trouble at all," Orville wrote in his diary on September 23, 1902, "when I noticed that one wing was gradually getting a little too high and that the machine was slowly sliding off in the opposite

Make Scones

Kill Devil Hills was far from town, so the Wright brothers built a shed with a kitchen at the camp. Orville taught himself to make scones in the kitchen. Scones are rich, buttery biscuits popular in England.

You'll Need
3 cups (710 ml) all-purpose flour
½ cup (120 ml) sugar
5 teaspoons (25 ml) baking powder
½ teaspoon (2.5 ml) salt
¾ cup (180 ml) butter
1 egg, lightly beaten
1 cup (240 ml) milk
2 bowls, a large and a small
Baking sheet
Knife or pastry blender
Fork
Wooden spoon
Rolling pin

1. Preheat the oven to 400°F (200°C).
2. Put the flour, sugar, baking powder, and salt in the large bowl and stir them together.
3. Cut the butter into small slices and drop them into the flour mixture. Use a knife or a pastry blender to cut the butter into smaller and smaller pieces. Mix the pieces into the flour. Once the flour looks crumbly and you can't see individual chunks of butter, it's mixed in well enough.
4. Put the egg in the small bowl and beat it with a fork. Add the milk.
5. Stir the egg and milk mixture into the flour mixture with a wooden spoon.
6. Lightly flour a large cutting board or countertop. Empty all the dough onto the surface and knead briefly. Roll the dough out evenly to a ½-inch (1.2-cm) thickness. Cut into square or wedge-shaped pieces. Try to make the pieces about the same size.
7. Grease a baking sheet by spreading a thin layer of butter, margarine, or vegetable shortening on it with a piece of paper towel. Place the pieces on the greased baking sheet.
8. Bake 15 minutes, or until golden. Let the scones cool somewhat. They can be served warm and are especially good with butter and jam.

Dan Tate and Wilbur hold on to the ends of the 1902 glider and run down the hill to start Orville off gliding at Kill Devil Hills.

Orville or poor Wilbur and Dan Tate watching with horror as they ran to help.

The glider was repaired and as good as new in a few days. Wilbur and Orville were already back to gliding when their older brother, Lorin, and soon after him George Spratt, arrived at camp. Lorin was thrilled to see his two kid brothers sailing through the air in the shining white glider. What a glorious sight! The glider made a number of record-breaking flights. Three glides were longer than 500 feet (150 m) and five lasted between 20 and 25 seconds. Wilbur and Orville were pleased with the glider overall. But every once in a while during a turn, the glider would slide uncontrollably down toward the low wing as happened to Orville. Because the low wing's tip would hit the ground and dig into the sand, the brothers called the mysterious phenomenon "well-digging." Being the glider pilot when well-digging happened wasn't much fun, as Orville well knew. The brothers decided to avoid turns, just making straight, level glides, until they could figure out what was causing the problem.

direction.... The next thing I knew was that the wing was very high in the air, a great deal higher than before." Orville quickly shifted his hips to change the wing warping, but things just got worse—fast. "By this time I found suddenly that I was making a descent backwards toward the low wing, from a height of 25 or 30 feet." The glider crashed hard into the sand. "The result was a heap of flying machine cloth and sticks, with me in the center without a bruise or a scratch." It's hard to know who was more shaken up, unhurt

Digging for Answers

As always, Wilbur and Orville tried to think the problem through, loudly discussing and debating all the possibilities. It must be something about the tail rudder, they agreed. It had to be. Nothing else was really that different about the glider's controls from last year. But what about the tail rudder? It fixed last year's problem of spinning out of control. The rudder definitely helped stabilize the glider during turns. But the rudder must also be causing the well-digging. The brothers decided to change it. They took off half of the tail rudder. Now instead of having two vertical rectangles of cloth, the glider had just one. It looked more like a fish's tail fin or a boat's rudder. But it didn't fix the problem. The glider still went skidding downward during some turns.

After staying up late one night talking about the problem with his brothers and George Spratt, Orville headed up to bed. He'd had too much coffee and his mind churned the problem over and over as he failed to fall asleep. The next morning he came down from the loft exhausted but excited. "While lying awake last night," Orville wrote in his diary. "I studied out a new vertical rudder." Over breakfast, Orville told the men what he'd figured out the night before. The fixed rudder worked fine most of the time, right? But during a slow turn when the pilot didn't level off soon enough, the glider slipped uncontrollably down toward the low wing (well-digging). Why? A buildup of air pressure on the rudder was throwing the glider off balance. The answer was simple—fix the problem by making the rudder movable, like a rudder that steers a ship. Lorin expected Wilbur to debate against Orville's idea, as was their habit. But Wilbur didn't argue; he agreed. Making the rudder movable was it.

The glider pilot already controlled roll with the hip cradle and pitch with hand controls. Every-

one worried that adding a rudder control would make flying the glider too tricky. Wilbur suggested they just attach the rudder control to the hip cradle. Then when the pilot used the wing warping to turn, the rudder would automatically be turned too. They immediately got to work replacing the glider's rudder. A single 5-foot (1.5-m) rudder was put on the back of the glider. Control wires were strung from the rudder to the hip cradle. The Wright brothers now had the world's first flying machine that could be controlled in all three axes of motion—yaw, pitch, and roll. Just as the new improved glider was ready to go, Octave Chanute and his assistant Augustus Herring arrived. They'd brought along an odd-looking triplane (three stacked wings) glider to try out. There were now six beds and cots crammed into the shed's sleeping loft at the Kill Devil Hills camp!

Everyone was amazed at the Wright brothers' 1902 glider. With the new movable rudder, the brothers made glide after perfectly controlled glide. Chanute and Herring's triplane glider was a disastrous disappointment, but the men had a good time anyway. The camp took on the mood of a fun vacation; the men enjoyed the sun, sea, and wildlife as much as the gliding and scientific conversation. In the evening, Wilbur would play the harmonica and Orville the mandolin while everyone sang and listened to the wind.

Orville and Wilbur knew they'd finally done it. The Wright brothers had solved the key problem of control. Their 1902 glider was their breakthrough aircraft. It was a stable glider that could turn and be controlled by a pilot in all three

Dan Tate and Wilbur (right) flying the 1902 glider as a kite.

Wilbur making a smooth, controlled right turn in the final version of the 1902 glider.

home to Katharine about a successful glide in 30-mile-an-hour (48-kph) wind, boasting "That was the highest wind a gliding machine was ever in, so that we now hold all the records! The largest machine, the longest time in the air, the smallest angle of descent, and the highest wind!" The longest glide had lasted 26 seconds, and they'd made several glides of more than 600 feet (180 m)!

Even after their guests departed, Wilbur and Orville remained at Kill Devil Hills to keep gliding. The brothers stayed until their return train tickets nearly expired. They finally broke camp and headed home at the end of October. "Before leaving camp," Orville wrote, "we were already at work on the general design of a new machine which we proposed to propel with a motor."

They'd mastered gliding. It was time to think about adding power. The next step was building an airplane.

directions—pitch, yaw, and roll. Human flight was no longer a distant dream—it was a sure bet.

Wilbur later wrote about solving the rudder problem, explaining that "with this improvement our serious troubles ended, and thereafter we devoted ourselves to the work of gaining skill by continued practice." And practice they did, making about 1,000 flights in those last weeks of October. Wilbur and Orville glided whenever it was windy enough and not raining. The brothers became skilled pilots through practice. They could even safely glide in strong winds. Orville wrote

FIVE

Building the World's First Airplane

On the train back from Kitty Hawk in fall 1902, Orville and Wilbur talked about adding power to their glider design. They decided to call their powered glider the Flyer, after one of their bicycle models. How much bigger would the wings need to be to carry the extra weight on a motor? What kind of motor would work best in the Flyer? How powerful would it need to be? Soon after settling back into their routine in Dayton, Wilbur sat down and wrote a number of letters. By 1902 horseless carriages were becoming more common and there were a number of automobile companies. Wilbur wrote to these new companies asking if they could supply the brothers with a lightweight gasoline engine. It needed to weigh no more than 200 pounds (90 kg) and produce at least 8 horsepower. No one wanted to take on the task. It seems that building a single custom-made engine wasn't worth the trouble. Or maybe no new automobile company wanted to risk being associated with the failure of some crazy flying contraption.

In true Wright fashion, the brothers simply decided to build their own engine. How hard could it be? Their capable machinist Charlie Taylor had already helped them build engines to run the bicycle shop's power tools. Taylor was put on the new task at once. A local foundry cast the crankcase, using the strongest aluminum available. Taylor built the parts himself in the bicycle shop. "We didn't make any drawings," Charlie later recalled between puffs on a cigar. "One of us would sketch out the part we were talking about on a piece of scratch paper and I'd spike the sketch over my bench." A prototype of the engine was ready for a test run in only six weeks. It sputtered to life, chugging out smoke and getting red hot, but it worked. The crankcase of the engine completely

← This sculpture in downtown Dayton, Ohio, is called *Flyover* and represents the Wright brothers' first airplane flight. The sculpture is the same length as their first flight on December 17, 1903, and its rising and falling form traces Orville's path through the sky on that historic day.

Rear view of the small motor installed on the 1903 Wright Flyer.

broke on the second test, thanks to frozen bearings. A new casting was ordered from the foundry and the brothers and Charlie meanwhile worked out the little engine's problems. By May, an improved engine was completed. To everyone's amazement, it weighed only 180 pounds (82 kg) and yet put out 12 horsepower. That was better than they'd hoped for and meant they had more weight to work with for the rest of the Flyer.

To hold up an engine the Flyer had to be bigger and sturdier than the 1902 glider. It had a wingspan of 40 feet 4 inches (12.3 m) and a chord of 6½ feet (2 m), giving the wings 510 square feet (47 sq. m) of surface area. It weighed 605 pounds (275 kg) with the engine. The landing skids were made longer and braced so they'd handle the extra weight. The wing camber was made a bit steeper than the 1902 glider's to give the Flyer boosted lift. The brothers stuck with the uncoated

Pride of the West muslin fabric for covering the wings, but trussed them together using extra-strong multistrand wire. The Flyer would be controlled much like the final 1902 glider with a hip cradle operating the wing warping and rear-rudder control, and a hand lever for the elevator out in front of the pilot. But both the elevator and the rudder were made with double-stacked surfaces for more control of the heavier Flyer.

Like the gliders before it, the Flyer wouldn't be completely assembled until the Wright brothers arrived at Kitty Hawk. But they worked on the Flyer's center section (where the pilot would lie) and the engine was mounted in the bicycle shop workroom. The Flyer's center section was so big, however, that it blocked the doorway from the workroom to the storefront. Each customer who entered the Wright Cycle Company shop in the spring and summer of 1903 had to wait for one of those crazy Wright brothers to walk out the workroom's side door and come around through the front door before being waited on. What in the world could they be up to back there?

Screws or Wings?

The Wright brothers were thinking about how to protect what they'd already invented. The brothers never imagined in 1900 that they might be the first to invent a working flying machine. Nor did they expect to make money from such an invention back then. But after mastering the 1902 glider, they knew they'd made important strides in the field of human flight. A lot of other people knew they were making progress, too. Wilbur's 1901 lecture to the Western Society of Engineers in Chicago had been reprinted and read by many people around the world—including competitors. Samuel Pierpont Langley had even had the cheek to write the Wright brothers requesting the details of their wing-warping system and their lift tables! And a French army officer was said to be experimenting with gliders based on the Wright brothers' designs. Wilbur and Orville didn't want other inventors stealing their ideas. They wanted to make sure they got the credit they deserved. With Chanute's urging, Wilbur filed an application for a patent in March 1903. The application didn't give specifics about a motor of any kind. The application was more for the glider and its system of wing warping. The U.S. Patent Office had received too many flying-machine applications from crackpots to believe the application. The office was rejecting all flying machine patent applications unless there was proof that the machine could actually fly. The Wright brothers' application was rejected. Wilbur sent in another application with more detail, but it too was rejected that spring. The letters of rejection from the patent office only served to fuel the brothers' sense of urgency. Once they had a powered Flyer, they reasoned, no one could deny them a patent.

Unknown to Wilbur and Orville, they still had a giant hurdle in front of them. In his 1901 lecture,

Wilbur said that wings and power were the solved parts of the human-flight puzzle and that controlling a flying machine was the only thing left to be figured out. This statement had already come back to haunt the brothers. Remember that they'd had to build their own wind tunnel to completely redo all the wing lift numbers. And they'd had to construct their own engine! Wilbur and Orville were in for another big shock when they started making the Flyer's last needed major parts—the propellers.

With the wing designs settled on and the motor in the works, Orville and Wilbur were ready to fashion the Flyer's propellers. It shouldn't take long, they thought. Propellers had been powering ships for ages, after all. From knowing the aircraft's weight, its wing area and camber, and the horsepower of the motor, the brothers were able to use their own lift tables to calculate the amount of thrust their Flyer needed to keep flying once it was aloft. All they needed to do was make propellers that could produce that amount of thrust. The brothers figured there were tables out there that gave the amount of thrust needed for ship propellers of different sizes and shapes. It should be a simple matter of substituting air-pressure amounts for water-pressure amounts.

Wilbur and Orville headed over to the Dayton Public Library to look up the ship propeller tables and equations. They didn't find them. After searching through all the information available about ship propellers and asking around, the Wright brothers made a shocking realization. No such tables or formulas existed. It turned out that ship makers didn't use fancy formulas to design their propellers. They just worked by trial and error. If a new design worked better than the old one, they used it. Trying out a bunch of propellers on an aircraft wasn't possible. The brothers didn't have the time or money to do that—and it wouldn't be safe. The other upsetting fact they found was that the ship propellers out there only had an efficiency of about 50 percent. That meant that only half of the ship motor's power was turned into thrust. The brothers had counted on at least 66 percent propeller efficiency when calculating the thrust of the Flyer (and the horsepower of the motor). Wilbur and Orville needed formulas that told them the design of a propeller that would do exactly what they expected. Charlie Taylor recalled that "they couldn't find any formula for what they needed. So they had to develop their own." It wasn't easy.

"What at first seemed a simple problem became more complex the longer we studied it," Orville wrote later. "With the [flying] machine moving forward, the air flying backward, the propellers turning sidewise, and nothing standing still, it seemed impossible to find a starting-point.... Our minds became so obsessed with it that we could do little other work." The Wrights' young housekeeper, Carrie, recalled that the after-dinner debates about the propeller design became especially loud. Charlie Taylor said the arguing went on all day at the shop, too. The brothers' ideas, experimental data, equations, diagrams, and notes about propeller shapes filled up notebook after notebook. The breakthrough finally came when

Modern propellers like this one aren't much more efficient than the propellers the Wright brothers designed a hundred years ago.

The two propellers on the 1903 Wright Flyer were behind the wings, making the aircraft a "two-prop pusher" design.

Wilbur and Orville realized that the old idea of a propeller turning through water or air in the same way a screw drills into wood was wrong. The Wright brothers were the first to understand that a propeller was really just a rotating wing. And no one knew more about wings than the Wright brothers! They reasoned that the same airfoil shape that produced lift in a wing slicing through the air would create forward thrust in a propeller. A propeller was just a spinning wing turned on its side.

(Think about a helicopter's horizontal propeller. The thrust it produces creates lift!)

Wilbur and Orville's propeller work resulted in propellers that were a little more than 8 feet (2.5 m) in diameter. The blades of the propellers weren't flat. They had a rounded edge on the forward side, like an airfoil. The brothers built the propellers out of layers of spruce, glued them together, and then shaved them into shape with woodworking tools. Recent tests have shown that

Propel It!

The Wright brothers had to design a propeller for their Flyer from scratch. You can build and test your own rubber band-powered propellers in this activity.

You'll Need

1–2 feet (30–60 cm) of wire (any wire about the thickness of a paper clip works well)

Large rubber bands

Beads, ¼ to ½ (6 to 1.2 mm) inch in diameter

Thin cord or fishing line

Scissors

Needle-nose pliers

Small metal paper clips

Pencil

Tape measure

Propeller materials: empty plastic bottle, cardboard, heavy foil, thin balsa wood, or store-bought propellers

1. Use the pliers to bend the wire into the propeller tester shape shown. It needs to have hooks at the top and loops on the bottom. You can more easily make the loops by wrapping the wire around a pencil, then slipping the pencil out.

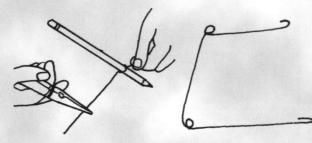

2. Make some 5-inch (13-cm) propellers. You can make the propeller from the "Fly a Top" activity on page 4 by following steps 2 through 4. Or make your own design. Make at least two different ones, but they should all be about 5 inches long. You can use a store-bought propeller, too.

3. Make a propeller assembly for each of your propellers. Unfold the paper clip, leaving one end with a hook. The pliers can help smooth out the unbent wire. Slip a propeller onto the straight end.

Use the pliers to turn the paper clip hook into a tight loop so that the propeller doesn't slide off but can spin when the wire is turned. If the propeller is too loose on the wire, tape down the tight loop onto the propeller.

4. Add the bead behind the propeller. Using the pliers, make a hook end. You may need to trim off the end of the paper clip. Repeat steps 3 and 4 for each propeller.

5. String about 3 feet (1 m) of cord or fishing line between two table legs, chair legs, or other posts. Make sure you have at least a foot of clearance above the floor.

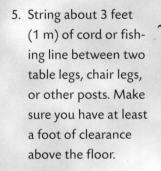
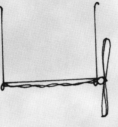

6. Slide the rubber band over the top of one of the wire hook ends of the propeller tester and down to the loop. Slip the propeller assembly through the other loop and attach the free end of the rubber band over its hook end.

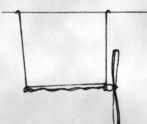

7. You're ready to test! Wind the propeller clockwise until the rubber band is very tight, counting as you wind. Hold the propeller still while you hang the propeller tester on the testing line by its hooks.

8. Let go. Measure how far it went. Then change propeller assemblies, wind the new propeller the same number of times, and test it to compare. Which one worked best? Can you conclude why?

the Wright brothers' propellers had more than 70 percent efficiency. That's very near what modern airplane propellers get. The Wright brothers' scientific research of propeller designs was one of their most important contributions to aviation.

The brothers decided to use two propellers on the Flyer. They calculated that two slower rotating propellers could move more air than a single fast propeller. The propellers were set up to turn toward each other, one propeller turned clockwise and the other turned counterclockwise. This balanced out the twisting motion caused by the propellers and helped the Flyer control roll. Wilbur and Orville didn't want the lifting surfaces of the wings to have to slice through air all stirred up

by spinning propellers. So they positioned the two propellers behind the wings. This made the Flyer a "two-prop pusher," because the propellers pushed the aircraft through the air instead of pulling it. The motor turned the propellers via bicycle chains and gears. Orville wrote George Spratt about their progress: "Well, our propellers are so different from any that have been used before that they will have to either be a good deal better or a good deal worse." There was only one way to find out. It was time to head back to Kitty Hawk.

SAMUEL PIERPONT LANGLEY

(1834–1906)

Samuel Pierpont Langley was an astronomer and physics professor. In 1880 Langley invented the bolometer, a device that measures the sun's radiation. In 1887 the noted scientist became the secretary of the Smithsonian Institution in Washington, DC. Both the National Zoological Park and the Astrophysical Observatory were created under his leadership at the Smithsonian.

But Langley became famous for his pioneering work in aeronautics. Langley wrote *Experiments in Aerodynamics* in 1891 and *The Internal Work of the Wind* in 1893. He spent 10 years testing different wing configurations with model rubber band–powered flying machines. After these experiments, he decided on two tandem pairs of curved wings, one pair placed behind the other. A small steam engine and two propellers went between the sets of wings. Langley called these model flyers Aerodromes, which means "air runner" in Greek. In 1896 Langley's model Aerodrome became the first mechanically propelled heavier-than-air machine. The 30-pound (14-kg) model flyer was catapulted into the air and flew for three-quarters of a mile. Langley's friend Alexander Graham Bell took the only photograph of the event. Langley's success prompted the U.S. government to grant the scientist $50,000 to build a full-size passenger-carrying Aerodrome.

In 1903 Langley was ready to test his Great Aerodrome. Like the successful model, the full-size version had tandem wings and two propellers. The wingspan was 48 feet (14.6 m), however, and the 53-horsepower engine ran on gasoline. The odd-looking aircraft was strapped to a catapult on a houseboat in the middle of the Potomac River. Charles M. Manly was Langley's assistant and test pilot. Manly climbed aboard the Great Aerodrome on October 7, 1903. After being catapulted forward down a track, the Great Aerodrome tumbled off the boat and into the river. Another attempt made on December 8 had a similar result.

Eight years after Langley's death, Glenn H. Curtiss (see page 130) successfully flew an improved version of Langley's Aerodrome. The first U. S. Navy aircraft carrier was named after Langley, as was the Langley Air Force Base in Virginia.

The 1903 camp at Kill Devil Hills had two sheds. The 1903 Wright Flyer is on the left. →

Back to the Beach

It was nearly the end of September by the time the Wright Flyer was ready to be crated up and shipped off to Kitty Hawk. Wilbur and Orville, now 36 and 32 years old, respectively, stood on the train platform in Dayton. As luck would have it, Bishop Wright was in town and went to see them off. Their father gave his two youngest sons a dollar. The 74-year-old minister told them to use it to send home a telegram as soon as they had a successful first flight. The bishop's boys promised they would and boarded the train. Once on board, the brothers began to talk about their Flyer. They felt confident it would fly. But would Langley somehow manage to beat them to it? Rumor was that the Smithsonian secretary was ready to test his contraption. The brothers doubted Langley's design, but he did have a lot more resources than they did. He had a full-time staff working on his Aerodrome and had spent $73,000! The Wright Flyer had cost Wilbur and Orville about $1,000.

The brothers were in for a bit of a shock when they reached their Kill Devil Hills camp on September 25, 1903. It was a mess! Winter storms had blown the entire shed two feet off its foundation. But the 1902 glider had survived in good shape inside the shifting shed. Wilbur and Orville got to work making repairs and building a second shed. Now they'd have room for the glider, the Wright Flyer, a workshop, and a place to eat and sleep. Luckily they'd just finished up the sheds when a four-day storm hit, bringing hurricane-strength winds and pounding rain. Winds reached 75 miles per hour (120 kph), tearing off pieces of the roof. So much water pooled under the shed that it even sloshed up through the floorboards. There wasn't much to do but hole up inside and dream of flying. But that wasn't so bad. Orville once said, "I got more thrill out of flying before I had ever been in the air at all—while lying in bed thinking how exciting it would be to fly."

Once the storm passed, Wilbur and Orville got to work uncrating the Flyer's parts and putting it together. They slipped the wooden spars and ribs

Wilbur and Orville at work putting together the 1903 Wright Flyer.

into the pockets sewn into the white wing-covering fabric. The brothers admired the smooth wings as they worked. "It's the prettiest we have ever made, and of much better shape," Orville wrote to his father. Assembling the Flyer took three weeks. When the winds and weather were right, they'd take a break and go gliding in the 1902 glider. The brothers wanted to give their piloting skills lots of practice before tackling a new craft.

George Spratt arrived at Kitty Hawk on October 23 and brought winter with him. Icy wind and freezing rain became the norm. The men fashioned a wood-burning stove out of a large metal can to heat the shed, but the water in the washbasin was still frozen in the morning. They took to sleeping fully dressed under piles of blankets. Being in a remote place did have its advantages, though. They didn't have to worry about hoards of newspaper reporters hounding them. The newspapers were torturing poor Langley in Washington, D.C., after his first attempt at flight ended up in the Potomac River. "I see that Langley had his fling and failed," Wilbur wrote Chanute about the first failed Aerodrome flight of October 8. "It seems to be our turn to throw now, and I wonder what our luck will be."

Misery Loves Company

As chilly October turned to cold November things were moving along. George Spratt had finished laying out a 60-foot (18-m) wooden starting track in the sand. The Wright Flyer was finally put together. It came in a bit overweight, about 70 pounds (32 kg) more than they'd estimated in Dayton. But the extra horsepower of the engine and the efficiency of the propellers should make up for the extra weight, the brothers figured—or hoped. They were now ready for an engine test. That's when the real trouble started. The engine ran roughly—it misfired, backfired, shook, and jerked. The vibration and jerking was more than the steel tubes attached to the propellers could take. The propeller shafts were badly damaged by the engine test. This was not as easily fixed as a busted rib or snapped wire. Wilbur and Orville couldn't repair steel tubes at Kitty Hawk. The propeller shafts would have to be sent back to Charlie Taylor in Dayton.

George Spratt volunteered to take the propeller shafts to the mainland and express-ship them to Dayton to save time. The young doctor was ready to leave the frigid camp by November 5 anyway. He'd come to see the first flight of a powered heavier-than-air piloted flying machine. That didn't seem likely to happen this year, Spratt believed. Spratt crossed paths with Octave Chanute on the North Carolina mainland. Chanute was on his way to visit Wilbur and Orville. Spratt told Chanute that he was worried that the brothers were in too much of a hurry to make a flight this year. If they tried flying before their Flyer was ready, it could be dangerous. But Chanute calmed Spratt down, saying that the Wrights weren't the type to unnecessarily risk their lives.

Chanute's third (and final) stay at Kitty Hawk wasn't pleasant. It was cold and rainy, and the food stores were getting sparse. They were still waiting on the repaired propeller shafts for the Flyer. The men made a few tries at gliding, but the weather and winds weren't right. Equally depressing were their conversations. Chanute was concerned that the propellers and engine might not produce enough thrust to make up for the extra 70 pounds (32 kg). At best there was no margin for error—it would produce just enough thrust to allow liftoff. After only a week, Chanute left camp convinced that there wasn't going to be a first flight that year.

With Chanute gone and the propeller shafts still on their way, the brothers tried to put their time to good use. The wood-burning stove that kept them from freezing hadn't been good for the 1902 glider. Its wood had dried out, which left it unsafe. But they could use the glider to test out the track launch system.

The Flyer was too heavy to launch by having two men hold onto its wingtips and run down a dune, as they did with the gliders. Besides, they wanted the Flyer to take off on its own as a proper powered flying machine should. Wheels would add weight and wouldn't roll in the sand. So instead, Wilbur and Orville had decided to lay down 60 feet (18 m) of wood rails on the sand. The Flyer would run along the track made of rails using two bicycle-wheel hubs. One hub was attached to the Flyer's front, and the back hub was attached to a little trolley that stayed on the ground. The brothers balanced the glider on the trolley and tried out the launching track. It seemed to work fine.

Problematic Propeller Shafts

Ten days after being shipped from Dayton, the propeller shafts finally arrived in Kitty Hawk on November 20. Wilbur and Orville installed the refurbished steel tubes on the Flyer and started up the engine. The propeller shafts seemed to be holding out, but the sputtering engine was making the sprockets impossible to tighten down. A

This is the propeller assembly of a Wright Flyer. It's sandwiched in between the top and bottom wing. The propeller shaft is the long tube that runs from the back of the propeller's center to the middle of the round toothed gear wheel.

healthy dollop of Arnstein's Hard Cement on the bolt and nut threads took care of that. Orville always said that the glue they used for bike tires could fix everything from a stopwatch to a threshing machine. As the anxious pair waited for decent flying weather to make their first flight, they kept testing and checking the engine. The Saturday after Thanksgiving, they noticed something was wrong. They shut the motor off. After looking over the propeller shafts carefully, they discovered that one had a hairline crack in it. If the shaft broke while in the air, it'd break into pieces, tearing apart the Flyer and doing who knows what to the pilot.

The Wright brothers realized that they needed to make completely new propeller shafts out of stronger spring steel if they wanted to get their Flyer safely off the ground. But it was nearly December, Langley was readying his Aerodrome for another attempt, and they were running out of time. Maybe they should give up. Their chances of becoming the first to fly seemed to be dwindling fast, especially this year. But in the end they decided to stay at Kitty Hawk until they'd attempted at least one flight—no matter the weather, no matter if Langley succeeded. They'd come too far and worked too hard to give up now.

Orville returned to Dayton himself, had new shafts made of spring steel, and was headed back to North Carolina all within nine days. Exhausted, he thumbed through a newspaper to pass the time on the train. In it he saw a story that woke him up. Samuel Pierpont Langley's Aerodrome had made a second attempt at first flight—and failed. His poor test pilot had been pulled out of the icy waters of the Potomac after the aircraft plunged into the river. Ridiculed by the press and scoffed at by scientists, Langley retired from aeronautics. When Orville reached camp on December 11 he told Wilbur the news about Langley. The brothers had mixed feelings about it. They'd never had much respect for Langley's design, so they weren't all that surprised it had failed. It was also nice to

Members of the Kitty Hawk lifesaving crew helped the Wright brothers launch their Flyer and witnessed the world's first airplane flight.

have the pressure of competition gone. But Langley's failure also reminded Wilbur and Orville that there were no guarantees.

A False Start

With Langley out of the picture, the only real obstacle left was the weather. Winter was only getting worse and the brothers had promised to be home by Christmas. The new super-strong propeller shafts were installed the day after Orville arrived back at Kill Devil Hills, a Saturday. The Flyer was a powered machine that was designed to be able to take off on its own from level ground. But the craft was overweight and with only 60 feet (18 m) of track to pick up speed, the brothers knew it would never get into the air without decent winds. There wasn't enough wind to fly that Saturday and even if there had been ample wind the next day, the two youngest sons of Bishop Wright never worked—or flew—on Sunday. Making the world's first airplane flight was not reason enough to make an exception.

On Monday, December 14, the winds were still too weak for a level-ground liftoff. But Wilbur and Orville couldn't stand to wait any longer. They decided to give the Flyer a boost by launching it downhill. "With the slope of the track, the thrust of the propellers, and the machine starting directly into the wind, we did not anticipate any trouble in getting up flying on the 60-foot monorail track,"

Orville later wrote. They hoisted up a red flag to signal the lifesaving station a mile away, as well as any interested Kitty Hawkers. The brothers had invited everyone to come be witnesses. The red signal flag was their way to say, "We're ready to try!" Five men from the lifesaving station soon showed up with two small boys and a dog in tow. Everyone helped Wilbur and Orville move the 600-pound (270-kg) Flyer and the sections of launching track partway up the side of Big Hill. Then they started the engine. The sputtering motor and whirling propellers made so much noise that the two boys took off running down the beach, followed by the dog.

Wilbur and Orville tossed a coin. Wilbur won and crawled onto the Flyer. He lay on the bottom wing, much as he had done in the glider. His hips were wedged into the padded cradle that controlled the wind warping and tail rudder and his feet braced against a small board nailed to the rear spar. Wilbur's left hand grasped the lever that controlled the elevator in front of him. The motor didn't have an accelerator. It only had two speeds—on and off. But the pilot could turn the motor off in flight with a kill switch, if needed, which had the effect of turning the Flyer into a (very heavy) glider. The Flyer's engine was running as Wilbur settled in, but it was held in place by a restraining rope. The rope was set free and the Flyer slid down the track as Orville ran alongside, holding onto one wingtip to help balance the aircraft. About two-thirds of the way down the track, Orville couldn't keep up. The Flyer was lifting off the track! Orville started his stopwatch as

Wilbur in the just-landed 1903 Wright Flyer on December 14, 1903. The unsuccessful flight broke one of the skids and damaged the elevator.

Four men from the Kitty Hawk Lifesaving Station, two small boys, and a dog help prepare the Flyer for an attempt at first flight on December 14, 1903. →

THE WRIGHT BROTHERS' 1903 "KITTY HAWK" FLYER.

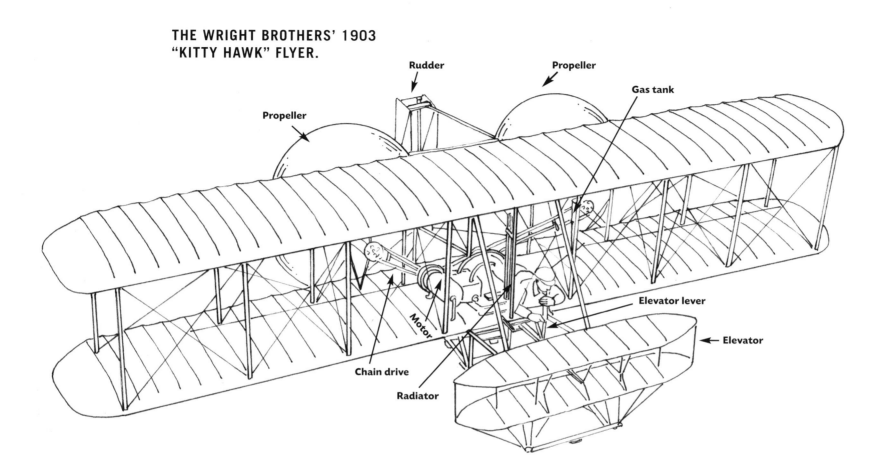

Rudder

Propeller

Propeller

Gas tank

Elevator lever

Elevator

Motor

Chain drive

Radiator

the Flyer lifted about 15 feet (4.6 m) up into the air. Wilbur turned the elevator up to let the Flyer climb, but the angle of attack was too steep. The Flyer began to stall. When Wilbur tried to level the Flyer out, he overcorrected and it plunged nose first into the sand.

Wilbur wasn't hurt and the Flyer only had a broken skid and a splintered elevator. It wasn't a true flight, but Will and Orv were as happy as the day Bishop Wright had surprised them with the flying bat. The Flyer had enough thrust to fly, the motor didn't explode, and the launching track worked! It just responded differently to the controls than the glider did. Of course it would, reasoned the brothers aloud. The Flyer weighed three times as much as the glider, after all. The crash landing was simply the result of pilot error. The brothers could smell success in the air!

First Flight

Wilbur and Orville spent Tuesday and Wednesday morning making repairs to the Flyer. As always, they debated and discussed as they worked. The brothers decided that the downhill launch had been a bad idea. They wanted a true unassisted takeoff for their flight. They reasoned that maybe some of the trouble Wilbur had experienced controlling the Flyer on takeoff could be blamed on speeding downhill on the track. The launching track was moved to a level area on the other side of the old shed. The winds died down Wednesday afternoon, so the brothers had to put the Flyer to bed for the night in its shed without trying a flight.

Wilbur and Orville got up early on Thursday, December 17, 1903. Like most other mornings at camp, they went about their daily routine. The men washed, shaved, and dressed in suits with stiff collars and ties. It was a clear day but very cold and windy. After breakfast they went out to take an anemometer reading. The puddles of rainwater on the beach were iced over. Wind speeds were about 24 miles an hour (39 kph). That was a bit stiff. The brothers waited a while to see if it would die down a bit. "The conditions were very unfavorable," Wilbur later wrote. "Nevertheless, as we had set our minds on being home by Christmas, we determined to go ahead."

The red signal flag was hoisted around 10 A.M. Wilbur and Orville started moving the launching track so it would face into the wind. They ducked into the shed from time to time to warm their hands at the little stove. By the time the track was moved, three men from the lifesaving station along with their two guests had arrived. The Wright brothers now had witnesses—and someone to help them set the Flyer onto the launching track. They started the engine. Orville set up his bulky box camera on a tripod so it was pointing to the sand and sky just at the end of the launching track. He slipped in a glass plate negative. Orville handed John Daniels, one of the lifesaving crewmen, the shutter bulb and asked him to squeeze it just as the Flyer took off.

It was Orville's turn to be pilot. He and his big brother shared a long handshake. One of the lifesavers recalled that "we couldn't help but notice how they held on to each other's hand, sort o' like two folks parting who weren't sure they'd ever see one another again." Orville climbed onto the bottom wing and settled into the hip cradle. The engine was warmed up, it was 10:35 A.M., and Orville was ready. Wilbur walked back to the witnesses shivering in the cold wind and asked them "not to look so sad…but to…laugh and holler and clap…and try to cheer Orville up when he started." Wilbur dashed over to the Flyer and pulled the propping bench out from under the right wingtip, and Orville released the restraining rope. Slowly the Flyer began to trundle down the track with Wilbur running alongside holding up a wing to help balance it. At about 40 feet (12 m) down the track, the Flyer began to lift up. Wilbur let go. The men cheered and Daniels snapped the picture. Orville Wright was flying an airplane!

THE WESTERN UNION TELEGRAPH COMPANY.
INCORPORATED.
23,000 OFFICES IN AMERICA.   CABLE SERVICE TO ALL THE WORLD.
ROBERT C. CLOWRY, President and General Manager.

RECEIVED at

Orville couldn't hear the cheers over the noisy motor as he hung on to the elevator lever and blinked in the frigid wind. He was concentrating on keeping the Flyer level. "The machine would rise suddenly to about ten feet, and then as suddenly dart for the ground," Orville later explained. The Flyer rose and fell, rose and fell for 12 seconds until it struck the sand 120 feet (37 m) from where it'd left the track. It wasn't far and it didn't last long, but it was the first flight. The men ran to the landed Flyer and congratulated Orville and Wilbur. The Wright brothers had done it! They were the first in the world to make a sustained, controlled flight in a powered heavier-than-air piloted flying machine—an airplane.

After warming up in the shed, the Wright brothers took turns making three more flights that morning. Each flight went farther than the last, as Wilbur and Orville got used to controlling the Flyer. Wilbur made the fourth flight around noon. He flew 852 feet (260 m) for an incredible 59 seconds, but a sudden hard landing damaged the elevator. The brothers figured it'd take a day or two to fix the elevator and get back to flying—yes, true flying! But it wasn't to be. While they were

The only photograph that John Daniels ever took in his life is one of the world's most famous images. Daniels snapped this picture of the first airplane flight at 10:35 A.M. on December 17, 1903. Orville is piloting the Flyer and Wilbur is standing in the sand on the right. The telegram Bishop Milton Wright received later that day is inset. Notice the mistakes made by the telegraph operator, listing 57 seconds instead of 59, and misspelling Orville's name.

Send a Telegram

There were no telephones at Kitty Hawk in 1903, but Wilbur and Orville were able to tell the Bishop they'd succeeded by sending a telegram—a message sent via telegraph. A telegraph sends messages along wires that carry electric current, called telegraph lines. These lines used to be strung across the country on poles, much as telephone or electric lines are today. Telegraph operators sent signals using a device that interrupted the flow of electric current along the wire. They used combinations of short (dot) and long (dash) bursts of current that represent letters of the alphabet to spell out the message. It's called Morse code. The telegraph operator on the receiving end, or a machine, translated the code into words. You can easily build your own battery-powered telegraph and send messages!

MORSE CODE

To send a dot (.) quickly press down and immediately let up on the switch.

To send a dash (-) hold down the switch three times as long as for a dot.

To make a space between words, just wait a dash length of time.

A .-	J .- - -	S ...
B -...	K -.-	T -
C -.-.	L .-..	U ..-
D -..	M - -	V ...-
E .	N -.	W .- -
F ..-.	O - - -	X -..-
G - -.	P .- -.	Y -.- -
H	Q - -.-	Z - -..
I ..	R .-.	Period .-.-.-
		Question Mark ..—..
		End of message .-.-.

You'll Need

Old magazines, notebook, or board (for a platform)

2 D-size batteries

Large metal paper clip

2 metal thumbtacks

2 rubber bands

Heavy tape (duct, electrical, or masking)

3-volt buzzer (available at hobby stores and electronics stores)

6-inch (15-cm) piece of insulated wire

Scissors

1. Set the two batteries end to end so that a positive (+) and a negative (-) contact touch. Tape them together so they remain touching.

2. Wrap the two rubber bands lengthwise around the batteries so that they cross on the contacts. They must be tight. If they aren't, use shorter rubber bands.

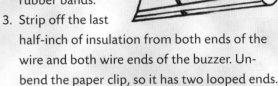

3. Strip off the last half-inch of insulation from both ends of the wire and both wire ends of the buzzer. Unbend the paper clip, so it has two looped ends.

4. Wrap the end of the buzzer's black wire around a thumbtack. Push the thumbtack into the platform. As you push it in, slip the smaller looped end of the paper clip under the thumbtack. Make sure the thumbtack is securely

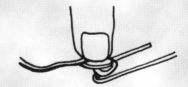

holding down the paper clip and wire. Tape it down if you need to.

5. Wrap one end of the 6-inch (15-cm) piece of wire around the other thumbtack. Push the wire-wrapped thumbtack into the platform so it'll be just under the larger looped end of the paper clip. Bend the paper clip in the middle a bit so the larger looped end rests ¼ inch (6 mm) or so above the thumbtack.

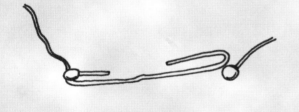

6. Bend the other end of the 6-inch piece of wire and the end of the buzzer's red wire into L shapes.

7. Slip the L-shaped end of the 6-inch piece of wire under the rubber bands over the negative battery contact. Slip the L-shaped end of the buzzer's red wire under the rubber bands over the positive battery contact. Make sure that the wires are touching the contact. Tape them down if you need to.

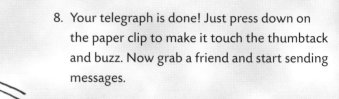

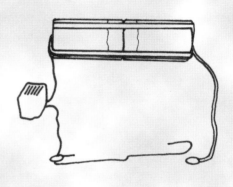

8. Your telegraph is done! Just press down on the paper clip to make it touch the thumbtack and buzz. Now grab a friend and start sending messages.

standing around talking about their longest flight yet, a powerful gust of wind caught the Flyer. It flipped like a hamburger and went rolling. Everyone dove and grabbed for the Flyer to try to save it. Poor John Daniels held on too long and went tumbling with it as it was smashed and broken. There'd be no more flying that year.

Wilbur and Orville were disappointed about the accident. But there was a lot to celebrate. They ate lunch and started the four-mile trip into Kitty Hawk. As promised, they spent their father's dollar to send a telegram home. It read:

```
Success. Four flights Thursday
morning all against twenty-one mile
wind. Started from level with engine
power alone. Average speed through
air thirty-one miles. Longest 57
seconds. Inform press. Home
Christmas.
```

Once back at camp, the brothers began to disassemble the broken Flyer and pack it into crates. Unlike the gliders, it'd be going back to Dayton with them. Will and Orv would be home for Christmas after all. The first airplane was their gift to each other—and the world.

The Missed Story of the Century

Bishop Wright did as his sons asked. He told the newspapers about Orville and Wilbur's successful flight, including some personal information. "Wilbur is 36, Orville is 32, and they are as inseparable as twins. For several years they have read up on aeronautics as a physician would read his books, and they have studied, discussed, and experimented together. Natural workmen, they have invented, constructed, and operated their gliders, and finally their 'Wright Flyer,' jointly, all at their personal expense. About equal credit is due each." How proud Milton Wright was of his two youngest sons!

Wilbur and Orville themselves wrote up their own statement about the first flights at Kitty Hawk and sent them to the newspapers once they arrived back in Dayton. "As winter was already well set in, we should have postponed our trials to a more favorable season, but for the fact that we were determined before returning home, to know whether the machine possessed sufficient capacity of control to make flight safe in boisterous winds, as well as in calm air. When these points had been definitely established, we at once packed our goods and returned home, knowing that the age of the flying machine had come at last."

Oddly, only a few newspapers ran articles about the Wright brothers' first flight. When Lorin Wright took his brothers' telegram down to Dayton's own *Journal* newspaper, the local publication wasn't interested. The Associated Press reporter read the telegram and said, "Fifty-seven seconds, hey? If it had been fifty-seven minutes then it might have been a news item." Those newspapers that did print articles were full of errors. The *Virginian-Pilot*'s December 18 headline read: "Flying Machine Soars 3 Miles in Teeth of High Wind Over Sand Hills and Waves at Kitty Hawk on Carolina Coast." Three miles over "sand hills and waves" is quite an exaggeration of Wilbur's actual flight of 852 feet.

Why did so many newspapers miss one of the most important events of the century? Years later Orville summed it up by saying, "I think it was mainly due to the fact that human flight was generally looked upon as an impossibility, and that scarcely anyone believed in it until he actually saw it with his own eyes." There had been so many hoaxes by cranks falsely claiming to have flown in some wacky contraption or another that people didn't believe the reports anymore. Hadn't one of the nation's most important scientists, Samuel Langley, just failed? If he and his $75,000 Aerodrome couldn't succeed, surely human flight was impossible, people thought.

The other problem was that those that did believe in the reports of the Wrights' first flight

12 Pages
In Two Parts

Virginian-Pilot.

True to the Democratic ...Party in Victory or Defeat

VOL. XIX. NO. 68. NORFOLK, VA., FRIDAY DECEMBER 18, 1903. TWELVE PAGES. THREE CENTS PER COPY.

FLYING MACHINE SOARS 3 MILES IN TEETH OF HIGH WIND OVER SAND HILLS AND WAVES AT KITTY HAWK ON CAROLINA COAST

TALLY SHEETS WILL DECIDE CONTEST

Chairman Dey Forced to Return From Richmond to Get Sheets For Committee

TREHY FACTION HAS ADVANTAGE THUS FAR

All Proxies Ruled Out of Meeting by Decisive Vote Before Fight Began

BOTH SIDES TO ABIDE BY FINAL DECISION

(Special to Virginian-Pilot.)
RICHMOND, VA., Dec. 17.

With all indications pointing to victory for the Trehy faction, the state democratic committee, after spending hours hearing the Norfolk election contest, adjourned just before midnight until 10 o'clock tomorrow morning, after a spicy session, in which some radical action was taken. Meanwhile Captain W. W. Dey, under instructions from the committee, left for Norfolk, accompanied by his two deputies and by Police Commissioner Reid. They are expected ...

ties he represented will abide the decision of the committee and always submit to lawful authority. With some ...

U. S. LANDING PARTY FINDS STRONG CAMP OF COLOMBIAN TROOPS

Natives Order American Flag Hauled Down on Cutter But it Stays Put

(By Cable to Virginian-Pilot.)
COLON, DEC. 17.

The United States cruiser Atlanta, Commander William H. Turner, returned here last night from the Gulf of Darien. She discovered December 16 a detachment of Colombian troops, numbering visually about 500 men, but, according to their statements, totaling 1,500 to 2,000 men, at Titumati, on the western side of the gulf, just north of the mouth of the Atrato river. The commander of the Atlanta sent ashore an officer, who conversed with the Colombian commander. The latter protested energetically against the presence of an American warship in Colombian waters, in so much as war between Colombia and the United States had not been declared, and politely requested the Atlanta to leave the gulf, because it belonged to Colombia. Commander Turner ignored the request, and the Atlanta ... to Colon to report to Rear Admiral Coghlan. The Colombians are clearly busy with protective and strengthening measures. Although they treated the Americans courteously they decidedly resented the presence of the Atlanta's landing party. The Colombian force was composed of the men landed recently at the Atrato river by the Colombian cruisers Cartagena and General Pinzon.

Early in the morning of December 15 the Atlanta sighted a small schooner in the center of the Gulf of Darien and followed her to the western shore, where the schooner attempted to hide behind an islet. Lieutenant Harlan P. Perrill, of the Atlanta, was ordered to board her and thereupon a whaleboat was lowered and pulled towards the schooner.

It was found that the schooner had on board a hundred Colombian soldiers, commanded by General Rafael Novo, who said General Daniel Ortiz, commander-in-chief of the Colombian forces of the Atlantic and the Pacific, had a large camp, a mile away, on the mainland. General Novo requested Lieutenant Perry to land and confer with General Ortiz. After temporarily returning to the Atlanta, Lieutenant Perrill went back to the schooner, which in the meantime had taken up a position off a beach within a small bay. Great excitement prevailed among the Colombians on the whaleboat's approach. There were repeated cries of "Viva Colombia," and there was a sudden concentration of about 150 Colombian soldiers on the beach. For some moments the situation appeared dangerous and had the appearance of ambuscade. General Ortiz appeared on the beach when Lieutenant Perrill went ashore, the whaleboat in the meantime lying close to the beach. General Ortiz insisted that Lieutenant Perrill should fly the Colombian flag at the bow of the whaleboat, or lower the American flag at her stern, because she was in Colombian waters.

Lieutenant Perrill replied that he did not have a Colombian flag and refused to lower the stars and stripes. General Ortiz did not insist upon his so doing, but he protested in writing against the presence of the Americans in Colombian waters. Lieutenant Perrill accepted the protest and conveyed it to Commander Turner, who handed it to Rear Admiral Coghlan on his arrival here.

General Ortiz and others freely expressed the determination of Colombia to fight to the bitter end in case General Reyes' visit to Washington is not successful and Panama is not returned to Colombia.

COTTON TRADE TO

TO DEEPEN THE HARBOR AT NORFOLK

Secretary of War to Report Plan to Congress For Making Ship Channel Here 35 Feet Deep to Float Big Warships

SENATOR MARTIN INTRODUCED MEASUER

(Special to Virginian-Pilot.)

Washington, Dec. 17.—Senator Martin introduced and had passed today a resolution directing the secretary of war to have made a survey of Norfolk harbor and to report to congress a plan, together with an estimate of the cost, by which there may be obtained a channel of 35 feet from deep water to the navy yard, and also the cost of a channel 30 feet deep. The channel is in places only 28 feet deep, and the department complains that there is always some fear that a warship will strike one of these shallows when coming into the navy yard.

All of the Atlantic ports are now clamoring to have the depth of waters in their harbors increased, so as to accommodate the increased size of modern ships. The need in Norfolk and of the Norfolk navy yard in this respect are as important as those of any other Atlantic port. Looking at the matter from a naval standpoint, the commandant of the Norfolk navy yard has for some time been taking a deep interest in this matter. Last spring Senator Martin, ...

"WANTS CANAL BUILT WITHOUT SUSPICION OF NATIONAL DISHONOR"

Senator Hoar and Gorman in Fiery Debate on Floor of the Senate

(By Telegraph to Virginian-Pilot.)
WASHINGTON, DEC. 17.

The senate today was the scene of a most important debate on the isthmian canal question as affected by the president's recognition of the independence of the republic of Panama. The discussion began with a speech by Mr. Hoar on his resolution of inquiry and lasted several hours. In addition to Mr. Hoar's address there were speeches by Mr. Gorman and Mr. Foraker. All three were notable utterances and of historical interest.

Mr. Hoar confined his remarks to his resolution, and they were carefully written out and read from manuscript. He held that this country has not yet received full official information concerning the isthmian revolution, and criticised in sharp terms the conduct of this country as shown by what has been given out.

There was no reservation in Mr. Gorman's utterances. He practically alleged that the situation in Panama had been created to make a campaign issue, and said that unless further light was thrown on the subject he would oppose the Panama treaty.

Mr. Foraker took Mr. Hoar to task severely for his remarks reflecting on the administration. He defended the administration for its attitude toward the Panama revolt. A heated colloquy took place between Mr. Foraker and Mr. Hoar during an effort of the Massachusetts senator to explain more fully his position in the matter.

Mr. Hoar said he was in favor of the isthmian canal, but was anxious that the canal should be built "without taint or suspicion of national dishonor."

"What we want to know is," he said, "did this government, knowing that a revolution was about to take place, so arrange matters that the revolution, whether peaceable or otherwise, should be permitted to go on without interruption, and whether our national authorities took measures to prevent Colombia ... ing a man about to attack another, is justified, before the blow is struck, in manacling the assailed party, and whether, after the assault has been made, the policeman is justified in claiming the pocketbook which has been taken from the victim by the assailant should be turned over to him (the policeman) on the ground that he was the rightful owner?"

Mr. Gorman took the floor as soon as Mr. Hoar had concluded, and there was from the start evident interest in what he might say. He began with reference to Mr. Hoars' speech and complimented that senator highly on his attitude and alluded to the democratic attitude on the canal question. On the latter point he said that democratic senators generally are as favorable to the construction of the canal as are republicans. Mr. Gorman said the facts were all that were desired, and he proceeded to refer to the extension of the executive influence, saying that that influence had been extended from time to time until "the senate had become practically the agent of the executive."

The affair in Panama, he declared, "was the most flagrant act of transgression that has ever taken place in the history of the country, and it should be resisted without regard to party."

Mr. Gorman criticised Mr. Loomis for his discussion of the Panama situation at a New York banquet before injunction of secrecy had been removed by the senate. Mr. Gorman said Mr. Loomis had discussed the Panama situation at a banquet at which perhaps many were excited by wine, and had "given information which the senate had not had from the administration or from any source. He did not," Mr. Gorman continued, "tell the country all the facts, but he made the broad assertion that the president was a bold and great man, who had had the courage and the patriotism to land marines and seize a part of the territory of the republic of Colombia, which we were under con- ...

NO BALLOON ATTACHED TO AID IT

Three Years of Hard, Secret Work by Two Ohio Brothers Crowned With Success

ACCOMPLISHED WHAT LANGLEY FAILED AT

With Man as Passenger Huge Machine Flew Like Bird Under Perfect Control

BOX KITE PRINCIPLE WITH TWO PROPELLERS

The problem of aerial navigation without the use of a balloon has been solved at last.

Over the sand hills of the North Carolina coast yesterday, near Kitty Hawk, two Ohio men proved that they could soar through the air in a flying machine of their own construction, with the power to steer it and speed it at will.

This, too, in the face of a wind blowing at the registered velocity of twenty-one miles an hour.

The *Virginian-Pilot* was one of the few newspapers to report on the Wright brothers' first flight, and its story was full of mistakes.

didn't really understand how important it was. Newspapers were using the words *airship* and *flying machine* to describe all kinds of new flying inventions such as helium-filled dirigibles. Many confused readers didn't understand the difference between a lighter-than-air dirigible and a heavier-than-air flying machine. So the news that some "airship" was flying around Kitty Hawk seemed like no news at all. They didn't understand the difference between Santos-Dumont's flight around the Eiffel Tower in a dirigible and what happened at Kitty Hawk. It's also important to remember that no one had a clue in 1903 about how airplanes would someday change the world. They had no way of knowing that the invention would one day allow people to cross the country in hours and send packages overnight. What's a flying machine good for anyway? people scoffed.

Huffman Prairie

Regardless of what the world thought, spirits were high at 7 Hawthorn Street that Christmas. Once

The Huffman Flying Field today (right) has been restored to look a lot like it did 100 years ago (left) when the Wright brothers were perfecting their Flyer.

the celebrating and holidays passed, however, Wilbur and Orville realized that they needed to make some decisions about their future. "We found ourselves standing at a fork in the road," Wilbur wrote. Should they keep working on flying machines as just a hobby, or should they turn it into a new full-time business? "We finally decided to make the attempt but as our financial future was at stake [we] were compelled to regard it as a strict business proposition...." In other words, the brothers needed to build a flying machine that people would want to buy. They turned running the bicycle shop over to Charlie Taylor and scaled back its operations. The shop would finish making the bicycles already in production and continue to do repair work, but no more new Wright bicycle models would be made.

Wilbur and Orville were already at work on a new improved engine by January 1904. The Wright Flyer II would have a better, more powerful engine and would be a bit sturdier. But where should they test it? Now that making flying machines was their new business, they needed someplace closer than Kitty Hawk. Besides, their goal was to build a practical airplane that could land and take off anywhere—not just on windy sand dunes. A Dayton bank president offered the brothers use of some of his land outside town. Huffman Prairie was a 100-acre plot conveniently near the Simms Station trolley stop. Mr. Huffman didn't charge Wilbur and Orville rent, but he did ask that they shoo the cows out of the way before flying!

The business-suited brothers became commuters, taking the trolley out of town each morning and then walking to Huffman Prairie. Their office was a big wooden shed they used as a hanger and workshop. "I sort of felt sorry for them," recalled Luther Beard, a newspaper editor who often rode the same trolley past Huffman Prairie. "They seemed like well-meaning, decent enough young men. Yet there they were, neglecting their business to waste their time day after day on the ridiculous flying machine. I had an idea that it must worry their father."

Perfecting the Flyer

The brothers set to work trying out the Flyer II at Huffman Prairie. But it was slow going. First they had to cut the tall tough grass by hand and lay out the wooden launching track as they had done at Kitty Hawk. Wilbur complained about their new proving ground's windless days, pesky cows, and bumpy field in a letter to Chanute. "While we are getting ready, the favorable opportunities slip away, and we are usually up against a rain storm, a dead calm, or a wind blowing at right angles to the track." While they'd managed to launch from 60 feet of track at Kitty Hawk, they just weren't getting up into the air in Dayton without those ocean winds. By the end of the summer of 1904 the Flyer II hadn't even matched the first Flyer's best flight time of 59 seconds. Frustrated, Wilbur and Orville decided that they couldn't just wait for windy days. They needed to find a way to

The 1905 Wright Flyer III.

launch the Flyer II when it was dead calm. Their simple but ingenious (as always!) answer was to use gravity.

The Wright brothers fashioned a tower out of four 20-foot (6-m) poles. A system of ropes and pulleys suspended 600 pounds (270 kg) of metal weights from the tower. When a rope was released and the weights fell, they pulled on a rope that ran under the Flyer's launching track. This rope pulled the Flyer forward and gave it extra thrust and helped catapult it into the air—no matter what the winds were. Now they were flying!

Within days after putting the new launching tower into service, the Flyer II had broken all the Wrights' Kitty Hawk records. On September 20, 1904, Wilbur made a complete circle around the field, flying for a minute and a half and covering more than three-quarters of a mile. The owner of a beekeeping supply store named Amos Root was there to see the world's first airplane that could fly in a complete circle, calling it "one of the grandest sights, if not the grandest sight, of my life." Root described the sight as a white-winged train climbing up into the air as it moved toward him. (Root was so impressed that he wrote an article about what he saw and sent it to *Scientific American* magazine. The magazine didn't print the article, so Root wrote about the Wright brothers in his store's newsletter, *Gleanings in Bee Culture*.)

By the time cold weather set in, the brothers had logged 45 minutes in the air. Once Wilbur had even circled the prairie four times during a 5-minute flight!

The 1905 Wright Flyer III circling above Huffman Prairie.

A Practical Airplane

Even with the launching tower, the Flyer II still had some problems. Wilbur and Orville set out to correct them in 1905 as they built the Flyer III. The biggest change was in the control system. While they'd moved the front elevator a bit farther out in the Flyer II, it had still been a bit unstable in flight. They'd had plenty of hard landings last summer. Like the final 1902 glider and the original Flyer, the Flyer II's hip cradle operated both the wing warping and the rear rudder. The brothers decided that they needed to separate the yaw and roll controls. They left the wing warping hooked up to the hip cradle. But the rudder on the Flyer III was now operated by a hand lever. The pilot had a hand lever for the rear rudder, another for the front elevator, and a hip cradle for the wing warping. Flyer III was a flying machine independently controllable in all three directions—yaw, pitch, and roll.

The added control seemed to make the turns smoother. But operating three controls made for tricky piloting and the summer of 1905 included a number of crashes. But after some tinkering and lots of practice, Wilbur and Orville were consistently making long, smooth flights. The Wright brothers spent more than 5 hours in the air in 1905 with Flyer III. They broke all their own records again and again. One October day, Wilbur flew 24½ miles (40 km), making 30 circles around the field over the course of 39 minutes. "I thought it would never stop," complained the farmer next door, who had been cutting corn when the record flight started. By the time he got to the end of the row "the durned thing was still going round."

The Wright Flyer III could now turn and circle with ease. The brothers even flew figure eights in it! It could stay up in the air as long as it had fuel. Flyer III was a flying machine capable of lifting off and landing again and again. Wilbur wrote, "Our 1905 improvements have given such results

as to justify the assertion that flying has been transformed from the realm of scientific problems to that of useful arts." The Wright brothers had built the world's first practical airplane.

The world's first practical airplane, the 1905 Wright Flyer III, on display in Wright Hall at Carillon Historical Park in Dayton, Ohio. Orville restored this Flyer and designed the memorial hall in 1946 that now houses it.

ALBERTO SANTOS-DUMONT

(1873–1932)

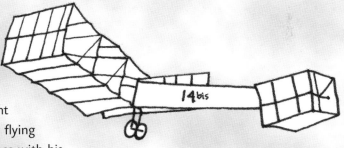

Alberto Santos-Dumont was a wealthy Brazilian inventor who lived in Paris, France. He was France's biggest aviation hero during the 1890s and early 1900s and his work inspired much of early European aviation. Santos-Dumont started out building lighter-than-air flying machines. He amazed crowds in France with his balloon and airship flights. In 1901 he flew a dirigible, an airship that can be steered, around the Eiffel Tower. The hydrogen-filled dirigible had a lightweight gasoline engine that turned a propeller, which allowed the craft to be steered. Santos-Dumont won a number of prizes and international fame for his Eiffel Tower dirigible flight. This was the airship flight that often came—confusingly—to mind when many people heard about an airship flying at Kitty Hawk.

While Santos-Dumont's dirigible wasn't a heavier-than-air flying machine, he soon turned his attention to airplanes. In 1905 Santos-Dumont built an odd-looking airplane called the 14-bis. Each wing of the airplane was a box kite and a third box kite was attached to the front of the airplane for control. In 1906 Alberto Santos-Dumont flew the 14-bis for eight seconds. It was the first motor-powered heavier-than-air flight in Europe. A month later he flew the 14-bis a distance of 722 feet (220 m) for 21 seconds. (Wilbur's best 1903 flight at Kitty Hawk was 852 feet (260 m) for 59 seconds.)

Santos-Dumont continued to design airplanes, his most famous being the 1909 Demoiselle. The Demoiselle became the world's first practical light airplane. This monoplane was only 242 pounds (110 kg)—less than half of what the Wright Flyer weighed—and inspired generations of homemade light planes.

SIX

The Wright Brothers'
Airplane Company and Legacy

Now that the Wright Flyer III was perfected, the Wright brothers had the world's first practical airplane. Wilbur and Orville had worked hard for years to invent the airplane, and they'd spent their own money working on it. The brothers had pretty much abandoned their bicycle business to concentrate on building a Flyer. Now they needed to make a living from their invention. It was time to sell their airplane. But who would buy it? Remembering that the U.S. Army had given Langley money to build an airplane, the Wright brothers decided to contact their congressman about their airplane. The brothers wrote that they had invented "a flying machine of a type fitted for practical use. It not only flies through the air at high speed, but it also lands without being wrecked." After giving examples of everything the Flyer could do, the brothers explained "it can be made of great practical use in various

ways, one of which is that of scouting and carrying messages in time of war." Wilbur and Orville were sons of a pacifist United Brethren bishop and believed that the airplane could help prevent wars. The brothers reasoned that if each side had airplanes and could see and know what the other side was doing, neither could gain an advantage. The War Department sent back a form letter saying it wasn't interested in experimental flying machines. They didn't believe that the Wright brothers had a working airplane.

Meanwhile, people were starting to take notice back in Dayton. The long flights in the fall of 1905 were catching the attention of more than just farmers and beekeepers. The local papers started to carry stories about the goings-on out at Huffman Prairie. Wilbur and Orville were in a jam. They'd invested a lot of time and money into an invention. They wanted to receive the

← Katharine and Orville Wright aboard the Wright Model HS airplane in 1915.

credit for it and make a living from it. But it looked like finding someone to buy it was going to take some time. And now that it was showing up in the newspapers, the brothers worried about someone stealing their design. After all, they had already had problems with inventors copying their glider designs.

Keeping Secrets

Wilbur and Orville made a drastic decision. They vowed not to fly in public until they had a sales contract for their Flyer. They would keep their design secret until they were certain they could sell it. It was a decision that caused the brothers a lot of problems.

Their old friend Octave Chanute thought the decision to temporarily stop flying was a terrible mistake and tried to talk them out of it. In fact, Chanute urged them to do the opposite—fly in front of huge crowds. This would make them famous and prove to the world that they had indeed invented a practical airplane, he said. Governments and companies would surely flock to them to buy their invention after seeing it in action. But Wilbur and Orville were convinced that if they did that, someone would steal their design. Wilbur wrote back to Chanute saying, "We honestly think that our work of 1900–1906 has been and will be of value to the world, and that the world owes us something as inventors, regardless

of whether we personally make Roman holidays for accident-loving crowds."

Wilbur felt that the airplane was an important invention that should be taken seriously. An article in the respected *Scientific American* magazine had just given them credit as inventors of the airplane. And they'd finally been granted their patent. Wilbur didn't feel that they should have to parade their invention in front of crowds. The brothers thought that buyers should believe them when they said they had a dependable airplane—even if they hadn't seen it fly. But after decades of hoaxes and contraptions such as Langley's Aerodrome, buyers were hesitant. No one wanted to sign a contract to buy a flying machine they hadn't seen fly. The Wright brothers contacted the U.S. Army again in 1907 but got another rejection. The army wasn't interested without a flight demonstration.

"We would be ashamed of ourselves if we had offered our machines to a foreign government without giving our own country a chance at it, but our consciences are clear," Wilbur wrote Chanute with frustration. The brothers felt they'd given the U. S. government its chance. Now they started courting governments in Europe as buyers. But government officials in England, France, and Germany didn't want to pay $200,000 for an airplane before they could see it fly either. Besides, their own aviators were making progress and might soon catch up. Alberto Santos-Dumont (see page 111) had made the first flight in Europe late in 1906 in his odd kite-box airplane. And who knew if these Americans were even telling the

One of Orville's final flights at Huffman Prairie in 1905 before the brothers decided to stop flying until they had a sales contract.

Orville (left) and Wilbur in 1905.

truth? Europeans—and an increasing number of Americans—were beginning to doubt the Wright brothers. If they had an airplane that could fly, why didn't they prove it? A newspaper in France voiced the thoughts of many, saying "It is difficult to fly. It is easy for the Wrights to say, 'We have flown.' They are either flyers or liars."

Competition and Contracts

The Wright brothers' sales strategy of not flying until they had a contract was costing them their credibility. Many in the scientific community, including Chanute, felt that the brothers were holding back the field of aviation out of greed. But Wilbur and Orville argued that they deserved to be paid for their invention. Regardless of who was right or whether or not their sales strategy was even a good business decision, it gave the competition time to catch up. The Wright brothers didn't fly for nearly three years while negotiating a contract. During that time, Santos-Dumont wasn't the only one to build and fly another airplane. The Wright brothers had serious competition right in their own backyard.

The famous inventor Alexander Graham Bell had organized a group called the Aerial Experiment Association (AEA). Graham soon recruited a number of aviation experimenters to his group, including the U.S. Army lieutenant Thomas E. Selfridge. The AEA had purchased a number of lightweight motors from a motorcycle engine maker named Glenn H. Curtiss, who also joined the AEA. A year later in 1908 Curtiss (see page 130) made the first public airplane flight in the United States. The short shaky flight wasn't anything like the long graceful circling flights that the Wright brothers had accomplished at Huffman Prairie three years earlier. But Curtiss flew his airplane, the *June Bug*, in public for all to see. An astonished crowd cheered as he was granted the Aero Club of America trophy.

However, 1908 was also the year that things began to look up for Wilbur and Orville. President Theodore Roosevelt had taken a personal interest in the Wright brothers' invention. In February of 1908 they finally signed a $25,000 contract with the U.S. Army Signal Corps agreeing to deliver a flying machine able to carry two men and fuel for a flight of 125 miles (200 km) at a speed of at least 40 miles an hour (65 kph). A month later they signed another contract with a French company. Both contracts called for demonstration flights after signing. It was at last time to prove to critics and nonbelievers that they'd been wrong about the Wright brothers.

Back to Kitty Hawk

The Wright brothers had put aside flying while waiting for a contract, but they hadn't put aside their Flyer. They'd been quietly working on a design that would eventually be the airplane demonstrated to the army and the French, called the Wright Type A Flyer. The biggest change was that instead of the pilot lying on the bottom wing, there was now a two-person seat. The wing-warping, elevator, and rudder controls were now operated with hand levers. The old hip cradle was retired. But before they built the Type A Flyer and demonstrated it, the brothers needed some flying practice. They put a two-person seat and the hand controls on the old Flyer III and headed back to Kitty Hawk. It'd been nearly five years since they'd made the journey. Their camp was a mess, but it was good to be back at Kill Devil Hills—and back to flying. It took a couple of flights to get used to the new hand controls and seat position. But apparently flying, like riding a bike, is something you never forget how to do.

The brothers once again made history in Kitty Hawk. This time it was the world's first two-person airplane flights. Dayton mechanic Charlie Furnas became the first airplane passenger. After a

The Wright Type A Flyer and Signal Corps Flyer had two seats like these—one for the pilot and the other for a passenger.

couple of weeks of practice along the Outer Banks, Wilbur got an urgent telegram. The French were tired of waiting and were demanding to see their contracted flying demonstration. Wilbur set sail for France without first returning to Dayton. The plan was for him to assemble his Type A Flyer after arriving in France. Orville went home to Dayton to start building a somewhat different version of the Wright Type A Flyer to take to Washington for the army demonstrations. It would be called the Signal Corps Flyer. The brothers would be separated for many months. It worried Wilbur. Could his shy younger brother cope by himself? "If at any time Orville is not well, or [is] dissatisfied with the situation at Washington," Wilbur wrote Katharine, "I wish you would tell me. He may not tell me such things always."

Wilbur Takes
Europe by Storm

When Wilbur arrived in France in the summer of 1908, he was greeted with skepticism. Who was this American bicycle maker? He claimed his airplane had flown for more than half an hour and could fly in circles. How could that be true? The French believed that they were the leaders in human flight. The first person to rise into the air in a hot-air balloon was French. Everyone knew that adopted Frenchman Santos-Dumont had flown his airplanes in front of cheering crowds. Now *there* was an aviation hero!

Wilbur was much less worried about the French's attitude toward him than the actual condition of his Flyer. When he opened the crates full of the unassembled Flyer he was shocked. Many of the parts hadn't faired well in transit and were broken. It would take seven long weeks to make repairs and assemble the Flyer. The job was made more difficult by a bad burn that Wilbur got on his arm when an engine hose pulled loose. If only Orville were here to help! "You can scarcely imagine what a strain it is on one to have no one you can depend on to understand what you say, and want done, and what is more, no one capable of doing the grade of work we have always insisted upon in our machines," Wilbur complained to Katharine. "It compels me to do almost everything myself and keeps me worried." Wilbur even insisted on sleeping in the shed that served as the Flyer's hangar. Wilbur and Orville had been a team for a long time. Going it alone wasn't easy—especially when Wilbur's assistants didn't speak his language!

Wilbur finally had the Flyer ready to go on August 8, 1908. The setting was the Le Mans racetrack. A small crowd of aviators, enthusiasts, and reporters gathered in the grandstand to watch—just in case this boastful American actually managed to get off the ground. The Flyer was hauled out of its hanger, set onto the starting track, and hooked up by a rope to the launching tower. Wilbur and his assistants checked over the chains and wires and then started up the engine. Both propellers whirred and spun as Wilbur climbed into the crude pilot's seat and grasped a lever in each hand. As always, this Wright brother was dressed in a business suit, starched collar, and tie. But he did wear a visored cap turned backward on his head. "Gentlemen," Wilbur announced without ceremony. "I am going to fly."

The launching tower's weight dropped to the earth and the Flyer rose into the sky. Everyone in the stands jumped to their feet as the Flyer took off. How could a machine lift off so quickly! Their own aviators suffered long lumbering ascents. The gasps of the spectators turned to near screams as Wilbur headed toward a line of trees at the track's edge. He was going to hit the trees! But Wilbur intended no such thing. He simply banked a turn, headed back toward the stands, and then circled again. No one in France had ever seen banked turns or such smooth flying. Their airplanes hadn't mastered control in all three directions as the Wright brothers had. *Très magnifique*! As Wilbur softly landed the Flyer near its starting point, the crowd rushed out of the stands toward him. They all congratulated him and shook his hand claiming that the American was a veritable birdman!

Wilbur made a second flight and further stunned the crowd by flying a figure eight! "The newspapers and the French aviators nearly went wild with excitement," Wilbur wrote to Orville. "[Louis] Blériot and [Léon] Delagrange were so excited they could scarcely speak, and [Henry] Kapferer could only gasp and could not talk at all. You would have almost died of laughter if you could have seen them."

Everyone at Le Mans that day knew they'd just seen flying as it'd never been done before. "The whole conception of the machine—its execution and its practical worth—is wonderful," gushed French aviator René Gasnier. "We are as children compared to the Wrights." The Wright brothers had done everything that they'd claimed they could. They'd proved the doubters dead wrong and everyone knew it.

"All question as to who originated the flying machine has disappeared," Wilbur wrote Katharine from Le Mans. "The furor has been so great as to be troublesome. I cannot even take a bath without having a hundred or two people peeking at me." The quiet, modest, serious bicycle maker from Dayton, Ohio, had become an overnight celebrity in France. People flocked by the hundreds to see him fly. Soldiers had to be brought in to guard the hangar and keep the crowds away.

Wilbur made more than 100 flights in France during the rest of 1908. The Wright Type A Flyer lifted up 60 different passengers. Wilbur's hostess, Madame Hart O. Berg, became the first woman to fly. Her husband tied a cord around her long skirt at the ankles to keep it from blowing up in the wind. After landing she had to hobble away from the Flyer in her tied-down skirt. Believe it or not, the "hobble skirt" became all the rage in high fashion that summer! Airplane madness hit Paris that summer. There were songs and books about flying on sale everywhere. Stores even started selling versions of Wilbur's odd visored cap.

The Wright Flyer Is Recruited

Back in the United States, Orville was having adventures of his own. He'd arrived in Washington in August and, as his older brother had feared, wasn't enjoying being the center of attention. "The trouble here is that you can't find a minute to be alone. I haven't done a lick of work since I have been here. I have to give my time to answering the ten thousand fool questions people ask me about the machine," Orville complained in a letter to Katharine. "I have trouble in getting enough sleep."

The demonstration flights for the Wrights' Signal Corps Flyer began on September 3, 1908, at Fort Myer, Virginia. The first few flights were short and the military officers and onlookers weren't all that impressed. After all, Glenn Curtiss

Aéroplane or Flugzeug?

When the Wright brothers invented their flying machines, there was no such word as *airplane*. They called their flying machines Flyers. People around the world soon started using the French word *aeroplane* to describe heavier-than-air winged vehicles powered by engines. Later, the word *airplane* came into use in the United States. Orville and Wilbur learned some French, German, and Italian while flying and doing business in Europe. You can speak some of the words they heard yourself.

ENGLISH	GERMAN	FRENCH	ITALIAN
Airplane	Flugzeug (floog-zoyg)	Aéroplane (AY-ro-plahn)	Aeroplano (ah-air-oh-PLAHN-oh)
Hello	Guten Tag (GOO-ten tag)	Allô (ah-LOW)	Ciao (chEE-ow)
Goodbye	Auf Wiederhören (owf VEE-der-hoor-en)	Adieu (ah-D'YOO)	Arrivederci (ah-ree-vah-DARE-chee)
Brothers	Brüder (BROO-der)	Frères (freh)	Fratelli (frah-TEL-li)
Wonderful	Wunderbar (VUND-er-bar)	Merveilleux (mare-VAY-yuh)	Meraviglioso (mare-rah-vee-YO-so)
Congratulations	Glückwünsche (GLOOK-vunsch)	Félicitations (fay-LEE-see-tah-SEE-on)	Congratulazioni (cone-gra-too-lah-zee-OWN-ee)

had flown the *June Bug* a mile in July and Douglas McCurdy had flown two miles last month! But as Orville's flights grew longer and he was able to showcase his ability to tightly circle, the crowds soon swelled to thousands. Orville was breaking world records nearly every day by the end of the first week. The youngest Wright was making flights of more than an hour and flying as high as 300 feet (91 m) in the air! Politicians and other dignitaries, including the president's son, started showing up to watch the flights. Word that the aviation age had truly begun spread across America and around the world.

"The newspapers for several days have been full of the stories of your dandy flight," Wilbur wrote to Orville. Wilbur joked from France that his younger brother was showing him up. "Whereas a week ago I was a marvel of skill now they do not hesitate to tell me that I am nothing but a 'dub' and that you are the only genuine champion skyscraper. Such is fame! Your flights have naturally created an immense sensation in

Europe and I suppose that America is nearly wild."

Politicians weren't the only ones hanging around Fort Myer that month. So was the competition. Both Glenn Curtiss and Lieutenant Tom Selfridge of Alexander Graham Bell's Aerial Experiment Association (AEA) paid close attention to Orville's flights. Orville was taking army officers up in the Flyer as passengers so they could experience flying firsthand. Lieutenant Selfridge was an officer so Orville agreed to take him up, too. But Orville suspected that as an AEA member, Selfridge was mostly interested in stealing the Wrights' design. Unfortunately, being accused of spying would be the least of Lieutenant Selfridge's troubles.

On September 17, Orville took off with Lieutenant Selfridge. After making three smooth circles he heard a tapping sound followed by two loud thuds. A propeller had broken, flown off, and damaged the rudder on the Flyer. "Quick as a flash, the machine turned down in front and started straight for the ground," recalled Orville. The Flyer plunged into the dirt, tearing the engine loose, and sending up a cloud of dust. Orville and Lieutenant Selfridge were pinned under the upper wing. Rescuers ran toward the wrecked Flyer's crumpled white wings. The Wrights' longtime mechanic and friend, Charlie Taylor, broke down in tears. He was sure Orville was dead. Orville was seriously—but not fatally—hurt. He had a broken thighbone and several fractured ribs, along with many cuts and scrapes. Lieutenant Selfridge was less fortunate. The rescuers pulled him unconscious from the wreckage. His

skull had been badly fractured and he died later that night during surgery. Lieutenant Selfridge had become the first person to perish in an airplane crash.

The news of Orville's accident reached Wilbur in France via cable. It only said that Selfridge had been killed and that Orville was injured. Would Orville live? wondered Wilbur. He immediately hopped on his bicycle and rode to a nearby town where he could send and receive messages from home more quickly. A return cable brought Wilbur the news that Orville was hurt but that he'd recover with time. Wilbur was relieved that his younger brother would be all right. But he felt responsible for the accident. "I cannot help thinking over and over again 'If I had been there, it would not have happened,'" Wilbur confessed to his sister in a letter. "The worry over leaving Orville alone to undertake those trials was one of the chief things in almost breaking me down a few weeks ago and as soon as I heard reassuring news from America I was well again."

Orville and his dog Scipio in 1921. Orville never fully recovered from the injuries he received during the airplane accident. He suffered bouts of pain the rest of his life.

The Century's First International Celebrities

Orville spent nearly two months in the hospital with Katharine at his side. The U.S. Army Signal Corps assured the Wright brothers that they wanted to continue with test flights. "Of course we deplore the accident," said Major George Squier. "But no one who saw the flights of the last few days at Fort Myer could doubt for an instant that the problem of aerial navigation was solved. If Mr. Wright should never again enter an airplane, his work last week at Fort Myer will have secured him a lasting place in history as the man who showed the world that mechanical flight was an assured success." Orville promised Squier, "I'll be back next year with a new machine." Orville Wright was not going to quit flying!

By the beginning of 1909, Orville was well enough to travel. In January he and Katharine set off for France, sailing across the Atlantic to reunite with Wilbur. The three youngest Wright siblings had quite a time in Europe that year. They went from France to Italy to Germany and on to England. Wilbur trained pilots and flew for wealthy dignitaries who came from all over the continent to see the famed Wright Flyer in action. ''Princes and millionaires are as thick as fleas," Wilbur joked. The trio was greeted by the royal family in Rome and visited by the king of Spain in France. In Rome a photographer flew with Wilbur and took the first aerial motion pictures. Katharine, Orville, and Wilbur were invited to stay at luxurious hotels and dine with Europe's elite. The Wright brothers had become international celebrities.

By the time their ship arrived in New York that spring, their fame had spread across the ocean to America as well. Five and a half years after their first flights at Kitty Hawk, the Wright brothers received a hero's welcome. President William Howard Taft awarded Wilbur and Orville gold medals from the Aero Club of America in Washington, D.C. Their hometown of Dayton put on a two-day celebration for its favorite sons. The entire Wright family was paraded through town in horse-drawn carriages. A choir of 1,000 children dressed in red, white, and blue formed a giant flag and sang them songs. Wilbur and Orville were presented with Congressional Medals of Honor, the governor awarded them a state medal, and Dayton's mayor gave them diamond-studded medals. At night a giant fireworks display featuring pyrotechnic portraits of the brothers was set off for all to see!

Back to Business

Truthfully, Wilbur and Orville were relieved when the hubbub began to die down. They had work to do. It was nearly time for Orville to go back and finish the test flights for the army. The brothers had an airplane to build.

The new Signal Corps Flyer astounded everyone at the flight trials that summer at Fort Myer. Orville and his passenger flew for a record-breaking hour and 13 minutes. As they landed, Wilbur was so excited that he did a little jig out in the middle of the field—even though it was his own record set in France that his brother had just broken. The flight test for speed was no less dramatic. The army would pay $25,000 for the airplane if its speed reached 40 miles per hour (65 kph). Each mile over that got the brothers a bonus of $2,500. Orville's passenger recalled that

This bench in Dayton, Ohio, carries the inscription: "Dedicated to the immortal spirit of Daytonians Orville and Wilbur Wright."

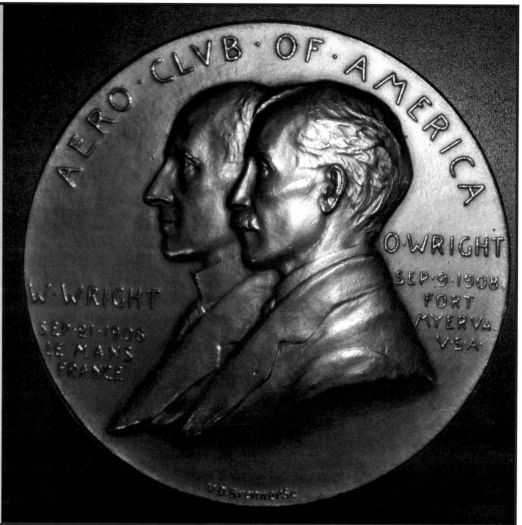

Memorabilia from Dayton's two-day Wright brothers' "Home Celebration" in 1909 is today on display at the United States Air Force Museum.

the ride was fairly bumpy, but their average speed was a blazing 42.58 miles per hour (68.5 kph). The U.S. War Department paid the Wright brothers $30,000 for its first flying machine.

After the trials, Orville headed back to Europe to fly and see about a company in Germany that was planning to build Wright Flyers. Wilbur headed for New York City where he made some of his most famous flights. These were the first true public flights of the Wright brothers' new model in America. In front of a million spectators, Wilbur flew across New York harbor and circled the Statue of Liberty. Boats and ships crowded into the harbor blew their horns and rang bells during his flight. Tears streamed down the faces of many onlookers as they exclaimed to one another, "Can you believe it—he's flying!" "It was an interesting trip," Wilbur wrote his father. "And at times rather exciting."

Late in 1909 the brothers formed the Wright Company. A factory was built in Dayton and by early 1910 it had started to manufacture two Wright airplanes a month. But people weren't lining up to buy them. Surely the machine was a marvel, people thought. But of what *use* is it, except as a toy for the rich and daring? To help promote their airplanes, Wilbur and Orville grudgingly started an exhibition company. Now pilots flying Wright Flyers could be seen at air shows, which were becoming popular around the country. But sending off pilots and crews without the painstaking supervision of the brothers proved disastrous. Six Wright exhibition pilots died in airplane accidents. Wilbur and Orville felt that the pilots

weren't being careful enough. They were flying like reckless daredevils to please the crowds and not maintaining the Flyers well enough. But the brothers couldn't run the factory and travel around overseeing the exhibition team. By the fall of 1911, there had been more than 100 airplane fatalities in the world. Eighteen months after the Wright exhibition team debuted, the brothers decided to get out of the grisly business. As Wilbur had said before, "I am only interested in

The Wright Company's airplane factory in Dayton, Ohio, around 1911.

How Fast to Fly?

In 1909 the Wright brothers' new Signal Corps Flyer aced the army's flight trial for speed by averaging 42.58 miles per hour (68.5 kph). That may have seemed blazingly fast in 1909, but it's very slow compared to air travel today. Jetliners cross the country cruising at 600 mph (970 kph) and even small propeller airplanes can speed along at well over 100 mph (160 kph). In fact, even most modern buses, trains, subways, and cars go faster than the Signal Corps Flyer could! The next time you're riding in a car, ask the driver to help you see how fast the Wrights' Flyer flew.

You'll Need

Car with speedometer

Cooperative driver

1. Ask the driver to tell you when the car is going 40 mph (65 kph). Does this speed seem very fast? Notice how quickly buildings and street signs go by. What would it be like to fly at this speed? This was the minimum speed the army required for the Wright brothers' Signal Corps Flyer.

2. Ask the driver to tell you when the car is going about 42 to 43 mph (68 to 69 kph). Does this speed seem much faster? Again notice how quickly buildings and street signs go by. This was how fast the Signal Corps Flyer flew in its 1909 flight trial.

building and selling airplanes. Let others amuse themselves with races if they want to."

Back in Dayton, the factory was building and selling airplanes. The newest model was the Wright Model B. The Model B became the world's first mass-produced airplane. It had wheels and didn't need to be catapulted down a launching track to take off. A single elevator was now in the back behind the rudder, instead of out front. While the Model B was very successful, by the end of its production run in 1914 it was looking quite old-fashioned. The truth was that once the Wright brothers had broken through the barrier of how to control an airplane in all three directions (pitch, yaw, and roll), human flight was out of the bag. Other inventors, designers, and pilots were soon building their own airplanes. While all of these were built on the design of the Wright Flyer, many eventually proved to be better airplanes. When Louis Blériot (see page 128) flew across the English Channel while Orville was setting records at Fort Myer in 1909, spectators saw a glimpse of the future. Blériot's single-winged monoplane had only one propeller out front and both the elevator and rudder in the back—the shape of the modern airplane. The Wright brothers had handed over their lead as aviation innovators.

The Wright Model B, or Wright B Flyer, became the world's first mass-produced airplane in 1910. It had wheels and a single rear elevator. This modified Wright B Flyer is on display at the United States Air Force Museum.

Legal Trouble

Perhaps Wilbur and Orville would have kept pace with the ongoing changes in aviation if they'd had more time for research and experimentation. But their days were now taken over by business matters and legal problems. Protecting their interests took up all their time. Some would say it was an obsession. "Orville and I have been wasting our time in business affairs and have had practically no time for experimental work or original investigations," Wilbur wrote George Spratt in December of 1910. "But the world does not pay a cent for labor of the latter kinds or for inventions unless a man works himself to death in a business way also," Wilbur complained. "We intend however to shake off business and get back to the other kind of work again before a year is out."

But Wilbur never did get back to the work he loved. Instead of spending his days happily inventing and debating with Orville, Wilbur now angrily argued with lawyers and judges in courtrooms far from home. While Orville oversaw business in Dayton, Wilbur was on the road fighting their legal battles. According to their patent, the Wright brothers owned the rights to wing warping. This basically gave the Wright brothers a monopoly on aviation. Anyone else who used wing warping had to pay the brothers a royalty. But many airplane makers tried to get around paying the royalty. They claimed that their control systems weren't exactly like those patented by the Wright brothers. Wilbur and Orville started suing

LOUIS BLÉRIOT

(1872–1936)

Louis Blériot was a Frenchman who made a small fortune manufacturing headlights and other accessories for early automobiles. At age 30 he put his money to work designing and building flying machines. Blériot made his first powered flight in 1907, teaching himself to fly an aircraft of his own design. Blériot improved on his airplane and soon started his own successful aviation company.

Blériot was declared a French national hero in 1909 when he became the first person to cross the English Channel in an airplane. On July 25 he left France in his monoplane, the Blériot XI. Alone in the single-prop 25-horsepower airplane with no compass, Blériot was unsure if he was flying in the correct direction. But after flying for about 40 minutes over perilous seas and through bad weather for 23 miles (37 km) he saw the chalky white cliffs of Dover, England. Blériot was awarded the £1,000 prize a London newspaper had offered to anyone who accomplished the crossing. His company also received hundreds of orders for the Blériot XI monoplane.

Blériot's company built aircraft for the French government during World War I (1914–1918). All the Allied Nations used his famous SPAD fighter biplane in the early part of the war. After other more advanced airplanes replaced the SPAD in combat, Blériot's airplane became a training craft. Many U.S. air service pilots in World War I learned to fly in a Blériot model airplane.

This flyable look-alike of a Wright B Flyer was built by a group of Dayton, Ohio, aviation enthusiasts. They take passengers on rides and fly the historic airplane at air shows.

aviators who flew airplanes without paying them a wing-warping royalty.

One of the longest of the Wright brothers' patent wars was with Glenn Curtiss. Within weeks of making his historic *June Bug* flight in 1908, Curtiss was notified by the Wright brothers that he was breaking the rules of their patent. Wilbur filed legal papers demanding that Curtiss stop making, selling, or exhibiting airplanes until he paid the brothers the royalty they believed he owed them. The legal battle with Curtiss would last seven long years. And there were many other legal feuds between the Wright brothers and rival airplane makers. The Wright brothers ended up eventually winning most of their legal and court battles. But they lost friendships and some of their sparkling public image in the process. Newspaper reports of the legal battles made the brothers look greedy. Many people, including their old friend Octave Chanute, became frustrated with the brothers' endless lawsuits. "Your usually sound judgment has been warped by the desire for great wealth," Chanute scolded Wilbur in a letter. The aviation community believed that the Wrights' lawsuits were holding back airplane development. Fortunately Wilbur and Chanute were back on speaking terms before the great engineer passed away in 1910.

A Genius Passes

Wilbur spent the winter of 1911 and 1912 in New York City testifying at the trial against Curtiss. It was exhausting work that Wilbur had to endure away from the support of his family. By the spring of 1912 Wilbur was mentally, emotionally, and physically exhausted. When would he get back to experimenting? He hadn't even piloted an airplane for two years!

When Wilbur caught typhoid fever from eating contaminated shellfish, his body was in no shape to fight off the disease. He became very ill. He was finally well enough to travel home to Dayton in early May. But he soon became worse, running a high fever for more than a week. Wilbur called in a lawyer to write his will. He seemed to get better for a few days after that. But he was simply too weak. Wilbur Wright died in bed at the Hawthorn Street family home on May 30, 1912. He was only 45 years old. Bishop Wright wrote the following in his diary about Wilbur after his death. "A short life, full of consequences. An unfailing intellect, imperturbable temper, great self-reliance and as great modesty, seeing the right clearly, pursuing it steadfastly, he lived and died." Thousands of people sent telegrams and flowers to the family in Dayton. More than 25,000 people passed by Wilbur's coffin to pay their final respects.

The entire Wright family was greatly saddened by Wilbur's passing. But Orville was devastated. Wilbur hadn't just been a brother. He'd been

GLENN H. CURTISS

(1878–1930)

Glenn Curtiss, like the Wright brothers, was a bicycle maker around the turn of the century. Curtiss was also a record-setting champion bicycle racer and his shop expanded over time to build and sell motorcycles. Curtiss became more interested in flying than riding through building engines for lighter-than-air dirigibles. In 1907 Alexander Graham Bell recruited Curtiss into his Aerial Experiment Association (AEA) group, and Curtiss started experimenting with powered heavier-than-air machines.

Glenn Curtiss's first airplane was called the *June Bug.* It won a number of prizes, including the *Scientific American* trophy for the first public flight of one kilometer in the United States in 1908. The *June Bug* was controlled by hinged flaps on the wings, called ailerons, instead of by twisting the wings as the Wright Flyers did. Modern airplanes use ailerons to control roll, too. Ailerons and wing warping both control roll by giving one wing more lift than the other. Whether or not this meant that ailerons were the same idea as wing warping and therefore subject to the Wright

patent was the focus of the long-fought Wright-Curtiss patent wars. Further irritating the Wright family was the fact that Curtiss modified and flew a version of Samuel Langley's Aerodrome in 1914. The Smithsonian wanted to prove that its former secretary deserved credit for inventing the first airplane, not the Wright brothers, and Curtiss believed doing so could help him in court with the Wrights.

Regardless of Glenn Curtiss's legal battles with the Wrights, he was a very important builder of early airplanes in America. In 1911 Curtis flew the first seaplane, an airplane that can land on water. The Curtiss Aeroplane and Motor Company built more than 5,000 biplanes for the military during World War I. The famous Curtiss JN-4 "Jenny" was the military's primary training airplane for many years.

Orville's best friend, his business partner, and his life companion. Together they'd been able to do what no one else ever had. The team of Wilbur and Orville had accomplished the dream of human flight. Now there was no "Wilbur and Orville." It was just Orville. "Orville was much affected by the death of Wilbur," says Wilkinson Wright, a grandnephew of the famous brothers. "There was unquestioningly a synergism between Orville and Wilbur. The sum of the two was greater than the individual parts."

The Wrights moved into their Hawthorn Hill mansion in 1914. Today it's owned by a Dayton company that hosts special events there.

Changes at Work and at Home

Orville and Katharine felt that the lawsuits with Curtiss had played a part in their brother's death. Orville vowed to go ahead with the legal battles—for Wilbur's sake. By 1915, most of the patent suits had been resolved and Orville decided he wanted out of the business world altogether. Orville sold his interest in the Wright Company. With the United States entering World War I and the military in need of fighter airplanes, the government took over the patents and paid the Wright Company and Curtiss Aeroplane and Motor a settlement amount. The Wright-Curtiss patent wars were over. The Wright Company was sold and reorganized a number of times after Orville sold it. In the 1920s as the Wright Aeronautical Company it was the most innovative airplane engine company in the country. In an odd twist of fate, the Wright Aeronautical Company eventually merged with Curtiss Aeroplane and Motor. The Curtiss-Wright Corporation is still in business today.

Wilbur and Orville had started to build a magnificent new home with their fortune before Wilbur died. Orville finished the mansion and Katharine, Bishop Wright, and Orville moved into the large house, called Hawthorn Hill, in 1914.

Change is a natural part of all families, and the Wrights were no different. Bishop Wright passed away at age 88 in 1917. Katharine and Orville continued to live at Hawthorn Hill with their housekeeper Carrie. They spent summers with nieces and nephews on Lake Huron's Lambert Island, where Orville tinkered with boats and made improvements to the cabins. Perhaps finally feeling the need for a life of her own, Katharine married in 1926 at age 52 and moved to Kansas City with her husband. Orville felt so betrayed by his sister that he vowed never to speak to her again. However, he did go to her bedside when she was dying of pneumonia in 1929.

Aviation's Elder Statesman

After selling the Wright Company, Orville built a laboratory and continued to do aviation research. He built another wind tunnel to test airfoil and wing shapes, developed an automatic pilot system, and worked on airplanes for the military. With the start of World War I came the airplane's first truly practical use—war. At first the airplane was mainly used to check up on the enemy and track its movements. But airplanes were soon fitted with

This group picture was taken in 1915 on the steps of Hawthorn Hill, the Wright family mansion. Orville is standing up, Bishop Wright is seated to the right of Orville, and Katharine is seated on the far right.

Field Guide to the Air

Orville lived to see all sorts of airplanes flying through the air, not to mention helicopters, jets, and rockets. Today you too can see different kinds of aircraft zipping through the air—jet airliners, military airplanes, traffic helicopters, modern gliders, and even odd-looking ultralights. You can learn to identify modern flying machines by making your own field guide.

You'll Need
Notebook scrap paper
Pen or pencil
Books about airplanes (see page 144)
Camera and film (optional)

1. When you spot an airplane, helicopter, or jet, sketch it or snap its picture so you can remember what it looks like.
2. Make a page for your aircraft in your notebook. Write down anything you noticed about it: Could you hear it? What did it sound like? Was it flying very high, or not too high? Could you see propellers or do you think it was a jet? Did it leave a white contrail behind it?
3. Use reference books about air travel to identify your aircraft. At first, just try to identify the general type of aircraft it is. Is it an airliner or a helicopter? A small propeller plane or a military jet? Once you get the hang of it, you'll soon be adding model numbers and sounding like an aviation expert!

Have you ever seen any of these modern aircraft?

guns and the era of World War I aerial dogfights began. Orville would live to see air power dominate World War II as airplanes bombed Europe, became suicide weapons for kamikaze pilots, and dropped the atomic bomb on Japan. It wasn't what the Wright brothers had hoped the airplane would be used for, but it was far beyond their control. "I feel about the airplane much as I do in regard to fire," Orville once explained. "That is, I regret all the terrible damage caused by fire. But I think it is good for the human race that someone discovered how to start fires, and that it is possible to put fire to thousands of important uses."

Luckily, Orville also lived to see many of the airplane's important uses besides war. The 1920s and 1930s were a real golden age of airplane development. Daring pilots like Charles Lindbergh and Amelia Earhart became household names and national heroes. New airplane models, made of aluminum with improved and more powerful engines, were designed. With better navigation instruments and safety features, airplanes could soon fly high enough to cross mountains and fly at night.

After World War II, traveling and shipping via air became a necessity, not a luxury. Letters to Europe now arrived in days, not months. Immigrants who traveled to America by steamship could now fly back to their childhood homes in hours. Aviation made the world a much smaller place to get around in. Orville also watched as the invention of jet engines made flying faster and longer travel possible. The year before Orville died, a pilot broke the speed of sound in a rocket plane. Orville had lived to see the beginnings of flight's next big step—from the sky to outer space.

As aviation's elder statesman, Orville's later years were punctuated with many award ceremonies and memorial dedications. The grandest of these was the Wright Memorial, which was built at Kitty Hawk. It is the only great national monument that was dedicated to someone who was still living. Orville traveled to the dedication ceremony in 1932 across the Wright Memorial Bridge that now connected Kitty Hawk to the mainland. He had become a legend in his own time. The memorial is a 60-foot (18 m) tower of granite built on top of Big Hill at Kill Devil Hills. Those at the ceremony noticed that Orville didn't look as if he were paying much attention to the speakers. His gaze often seemed focused on faraway dunes or on the horizon line of sky and water.

Perhaps Orville was thinking about that first flight back on a frigid December morning in 1903. Or perhaps he was remembering a different kind of historic day back in May of 1910. The factory

was then newly built and trips out to the testing field at Huffman Prairie were still routine. But this wasn't a routine day. With the brothers on the familiar trolley trip was their father, 81-year-old Bishop Wright. The three Wright men walked from Simms Station to the hangar. The spring grass was bright green and smelled newly cut. Bishop Wright watched his two sons prepare the new Model B for flight. These famous men had lived in his home their entire lives. The bishop had asked that they never fly together. It would be too

Colonel Charles Lindbergh (right) visited aviation's elder statesman Orville Wright (far left) at Wright Field in Dayton, Ohio, in 1927. Wright Field eventually became Wright-Patterson Air Force Base. John F. Curry is in the center.

Historical Ohioans Stephen Wright on left (grandnephew of Wilbur and Orville Wright), John Glenn in center (first American to orbit Earth), and Neil Armstrong on right (first person on the moon) attend the presentation of Ohio's commemorative quarter that reads, "Birthplace of Aviation Pioneers." When Armstrong stepped onto the moon in 1969 he had a piece of the wing-covering fabric from the first Wright Flyer tucked inside his spacesuit.

The Wright family gravesite at Woodland Cemetery and Arboretum in Dayton, Ohio. Wilbur and Orville are buried here alongside their parents and sister Katharine.

great a loss to the world if they should both perish in an accident. But this was a special day. The brothers climbed into the Flyer and took off with Orville as pilot. It was a short flight and the only one they'd ever make together. Then it was the bishop's turn. The father of the inventors of the airplane had never flown before, but now he wanted to. With his youngest son as pilot, the bishop climbed into the air. Orville wanted his elderly father to feel safe, so he didn't fly too high. But Bishop Wright smiled wide as the wind whipped his gray beard. Then he leaned over to his son and cried, "Higher, Orville! Higher!" After all, he was a Wright, too.

When asked what he thought of the memorial, Orville said, "I think Will would have liked it." Orville lived the rest of his life at Hawthorn Hill. One day in January of 1948, while tinkering with a broken doorbell, Orville had a heart attack. He died a few days later, January 30, in the hospital. Orville Wright, the first person to fly an airplane, was 77 years old.

The Fate of the
Wright "Kitty Hawk" Flyer

What ever became of the world's first airplane? Today the Wright "Kitty Hawk" 1903 Flyer is suspended from the ceiling at the Smithsonian Institution's National Air and Space Museum. It greets visitors as they enter the Milestones of Flight Gallery. But the Flyer didn't go to the Smithsonian until after Orville died. In fact, the world's first airplane nearly didn't survive at all.

The first Flyer was smashed by a gust of wind on the first and only day it ever flew—December 17, 1903. Luckily, Wilbur and Orville decided it was worth packing up and shipping back to Dayton. (The three gliders were not saved.) The crates holding the Flyer were stored in a shed behind the bicycle shop and went untouched for 10 years. During the devastating Dayton flood of 1913 the crates were underwater for weeks, then moved to a barn. It wasn't until the summer of 1916 that Orville decided to repair and reassemble the orig-

inal Flyer for exhibition. The youngest Wright brother had to replace most of the rudder and elevator, repair the broken spars and ribs, and re-cover the wings with new fabric. Orville exhibited the rebuilt Flyer at a number of air shows and universities until 1928. That year Orville spruced up the Flyer again and sent it to the Science Museum in London, where it was exhibited for 20 years.

Why did Orville send the world's first airplane, which was invented by Americans, to Europe? It was Orville's way of protesting against the Smithsonian's refusal to recognize that he and Wilbur had made the first successful airplane flight. For nearly 40 years, the Smithsonian claimed that their own Samuel Pierpont Langley invented the airplane. For many years Langely's Aerodrome was displayed in the Smithsonian with the sign: "The first man-carrying aeroplane in the history of the world capable of sustained free flight." Finally in 1942 the Smithsonian publicly stated that the Wright brothers were the true inventors of the airplane. After that, Orville said that the Flyer could be returned to America. Because of World War II, the Flyer didn't make it out of Europe for a number of years. It was donated to the Smithsonian on the 45th anniversary of first flight, December 17, 1948.

The Flyer's plaque reads:

THE ORIGINAL WRIGHT BROTHERS AEROPLANE
THE WORLD'S FIRST POWER-DRIVEN,
HEAVIER-THAN-AIR MACHINE IN WHICH MAN
MADE FREE, CONTROLLED, AND SUSTAINED FLIGHT
INVENTED AND BUILT BY WILBUR AND ORVILLE WRIGHT
FLOWN BY THEM AT KITTY HAWK, NORTH CAROLINA
DECEMBER 17, 1903
BY ORIGINAL SCIENTIFIC RESEARCH THE WRIGHT BROTHERS
DISCOVERED THE PRINCIPLES OF HUMAN FLIGHT
AS INVENTORS, BUILDERS, AND FLYERS THEY
FURTHER DEVELOPED THE AEROPLANE,
TAUGHT MAN TO FLY, AND OPENED
THE ERA OF AVIATION

The Wright Brothers Memorial on the Wright-Patterson Air Force Base in Dayton, Ohio, sits atop a hill that overlooks Huffman Prairie. Its inscription begins, "In commemoration of the courage, perseverance, and achievements of Wilbur and Orville Wright...."

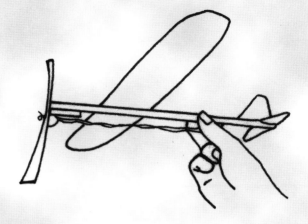

APPENDIX

Build a Powered Flyer

Now it's your turn to put it all together—just as Wilbur and Orville did. Use all you've learned to build a real powered flying machine. This rubber band–powered model airplane will actually fly!

(Note: You can also add power to the glider you built in the "Glide a Glider" activity on page 48. Just skip to step 7.)

You'll Need
Photocopy of the pattern on page 140 or tracing paper
12 x 4 inch (30 x 10 cm) sheet of ¹⁄₁₆-inch-thick (1.5 mm) balsa wood
Scissors or craft knife
Ruler
Pencil or pen
11 inch (28 cm) long ¼-inch (6 mm) square balsa wood rod

1 inch (2.5 cm) long ¼-inch (6 mm) square balsa wood rod
Large rubber band
¼–½ inch (6–12 mm) diameter bead
Needle-nose pliers
Small metal paper clip
Small eye hook
Tape
Glue
Staple
Newspaper
Propeller (Use one from "Propel It!" on page 90 or a 5-inch (13 cm) store-bought one.)

1. Trace or photocopy the pattern on page 140. Cut out the three pattern pieces and arrange them on the sheet of balsa wood. Use scissors or a craft knife to cut out the pieces.

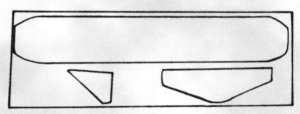

2. Use the ruler and pencil to measure and mark these distances from one end of the balsa wood rod: 2 inches (5 cm), 4 inches (10 cm), 8¾ inches (22.2 cm), and 9¾ (24.8 cm) inches. Write WING between the 2-and 4-inch marks. Write rudder at the 8¾-inch mark and ELEVATOR behind the 9¾-inch mark.

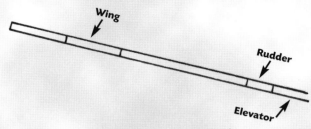

Wing

Rudder

Elevator

3. Very gently bend the wing piece, as shown. Keep bending and releasing it until the ends angle up a bit.

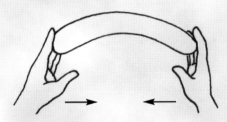

4. Set the rod on some newspaper. Glue the small 1-inch (2.5 cm) piece of rod onto one end, as shown.

5. Put glue where you wrote WING and glue the wing piece down. Put glue where you wrote ELEVATOR and glue the elevator down. Put glue along the notched bottom of the rudder and place it where you wrote RUDDER. It fits over the elevator. Glue around all the rudder's edges. (Use strips of tape to support the rudder if it keeps falling over while drying. You can take the tape off later.)

6. Let all the glue dry completely, reapplying at least

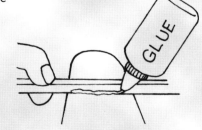

once from both the top and bottom, as shown.

7. Make a propeller assembly. Unfold the paper clip, leaving one end with a hook. The pliers can help smooth out the wire. Slip the propeller onto the straight end. Use the pliers to turn the paper clip hook into a tight loop so that the propeller doesn't slide off, but spins when the wire is turned. If the propeller is too loose on the wire, tape down the wire loop onto the propeller.

8. Add the bead behind the propeller. Using the pliers, make a hook end. You may need to trim off the end of the paper clip using the pliers' cutting tool.

9. Screw the eye hook into the bottom of the short rod about ¼ inch from the end, as shown.

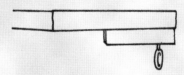

10. Insert the propeller assembly's hooked end through the eye hook. Attach the rubber band onto the hook. Pull the rubber band out straight

along the rod. Push a staple into the soft balsa wood to secure the end of the rubber band, as shown.

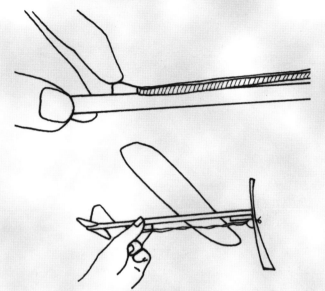

11. You're ready to fly! Find an open area. Wind the propeller clockwise until the rubber band is very tight. Hold the propeller still with one hand while grasping the flyer in the other hand along the rod. Gently toss it forward into the air as you let go of the propeller.

139

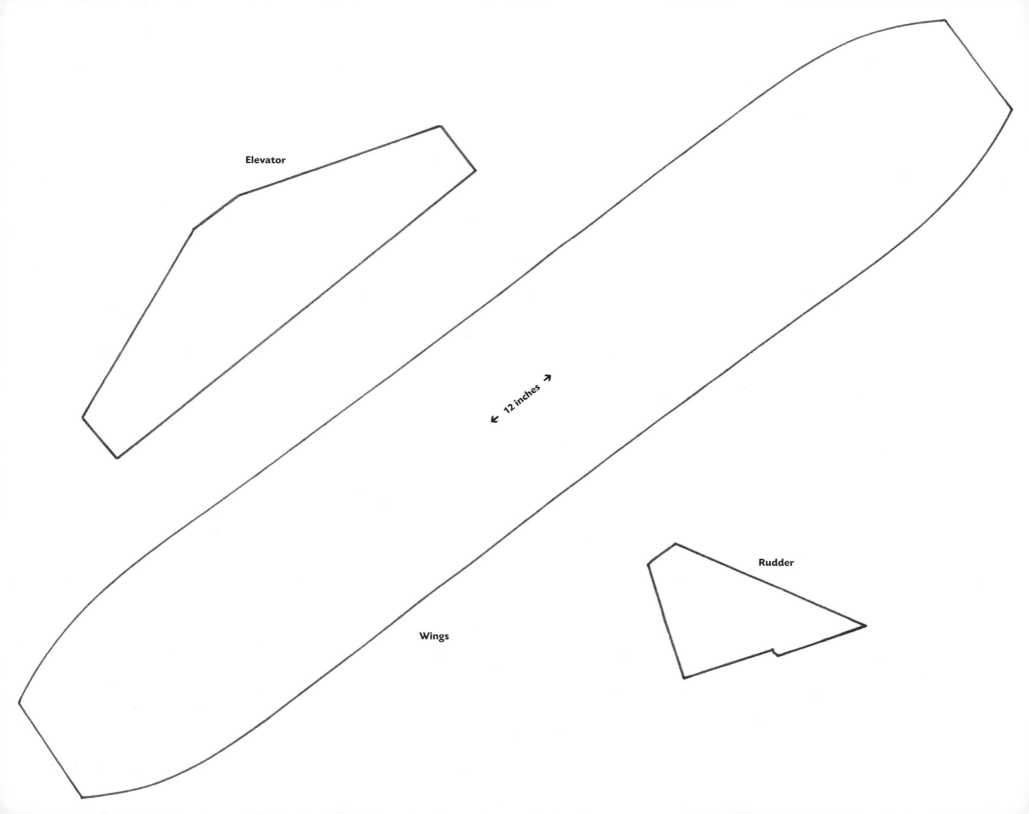

Elevator

12 inches →

Wings

Rudder

Glossary

aerodynamics — the study of moving air (and other gases), especially how objects move through air.

aeronautics — the science of flight and aircraft design, construction, and operation.

aileron — a movable flap on an airplane wing that controls roll (tilt and balance) and allows the airplane to bank turns.

aircraft — any vehicle that can fly, including gliders, airplanes, helicopters, hot-air balloons, etc.

airfoil — the curved shape of a wing that creates lift as it moves through air.

air pressure — the pressing force of air from its weight (the atmosphere) and also its movement (wind).

airship — a lighter-than-air, powered, maneuverable aircraft that uses a hot air–, helium-, or hydrogen-filled bag.

angle of attack — the angle of the wing's leading edge into moving air.

Bernoulli's Principle — a scientific law that says that as air moves faster, its pressure decreases.

biplane — an aircraft with two main wings stacked one above the other.

camber — the steepness of the curve of a wing's upper surface.

chord — the width of a wing, or the distance from the front to the rear edge.

crankcase — the metal casing that encloses the crankshaft in an engine.

dirigible — a lighter-than-air aircraft or airship with its own power and steering.

drag — the force that acts against an aircraft's forward force (thrust) and is caused by friction between the air and the aircraft.

elevator — a movable horizontal surface on an airplane that controls pitch (up and down movement).

fixed-wing aircraft — an aircraft with wings that don't move or flap.

force — a push or pull on an object that tends to make it change speed, position, or direction.

friction — the rubbing of two objects against each other.

fuselage — the main body of an airplane, including the pilot cockpit, passenger seating, and cargo area but not the wings.

glider — an aircraft with no engine or power that flies by riding air currents alone; an unpowered airplane.

gravity — the force that pulls all objects down toward earth.

gyroscope — a rotating metal wheel inside a circular frame that turns while the wheel spins in place.

heavier-than-air flight — flight in aircraft that weigh more than air, like airplanes, gliders, and helicopters.

helicopter — an aircraft without wings that flies vertically and horizontally by spinning large blades above it.

horizontal — in line with, or parallel to, the horizon; lying down.

hot-air balloon — a bag filled with heated gas or air that floats.

jet engine — an aircraft engine that uses oxygen to burn fuel and shoots out heated air and exhaust gases that propel it forward.

lift — a force that pushes upward against gravity.

lift coefficient — the amount of lift a particular shaped airfoil produces at a specific angle of attack.

lift tables — lists of lift (and drag) amounts, or coefficients, for specific airfoil shapes and angles of attack.

lighter-than-air flight — flight in floating aircraft that weigh less than air, like hot-air balloons, airships, and dirigibles.

monoplane — an aircraft with one main wing

Newton's Third Law of Motion — the scientific law that says that for every action there is an equal and opposite reaction.

ornithology — the scientific study of birds.

ornithopter — a flying machine that has flapping wings.

pitch — the up and down (climbing and diving) direction of movement of an aircraft.

propeller — an airfoil that an engine turns to provide thrust, pulling the airplane through the air.

ribs — short support bars that run from the front to the back of a wing between spars.

rocket engine — an engine that produces great amounts of thrust by burning both fuel and oxygen and shooting the hot gases created through a nozzle.

roll — the tilt and balance direction of movement of an aircraft.

rudder — a movable vertical surface on an airplane that controls yaw (left and right movement).

spar — long support bars that run the length of an aircraft's wing.

stall — when an aircraft slows down to the point where the wing stops producing lift, often because the angle of attack is too steep.

strut — support bars that connect the two stacked wings of a biplane and are often trussed with wire.

thrust — the forward force of a flying aircraft.

triplane — an aircraft with three main wings stacked one above the other.

truss — wire that gives support to aircraft wings.

vertical — at a right angle to, or perpendicular to, the horizon; upright.

wing — part of the airplane shaped like an airfoil that creates lift when air flows over it.

wing warping — a system of roll control invented by the Wright brothers that uses wires to twist or warp the wings to give one side of the wings more lift than the other, allowing stable banked turns.

wingspan — the length of a wing; the distance from one wingtip to the other.

yaw — the left and right direction of movement of an aircraft.

Web Sites to Explore

American Experience: The Wright Stuff
www.pbs.org/wgbh/amex/wright
Listen to interviews, watch film clips, and read the transcript from the American Experience documentary about the Wright brothers.

Aviation Pioneers: An Anthology
www.ctie.monash.edu.au/hargrave/pioneers.html
"Saluting the men and women of aviation history" is this site's motto and it lives up to it. Biographies of pioneers of flight, airplane manufacturing, and daring aviators are featured.

Evolution of Flight
www.flight100.org
This American Institute of Aeronautics Web site has a great information-packed History of Flight time line and lots of fun interactive activities, including a Wright Flyer Simulator, in the Click & Learn section.

First Flight
firstflight.open.ac.uk
At this site you can experience a multimedia wind tunnel and bicycle balance experiments, while learning how Wilbur and Orville invented the airplane.

Flights of Inspiration
sln.fi.edu/flights
Learn about the Wright brothers, get ideas for fun hands-on activities, and also learn about the first nonstop transatlantic flight at this Franklin Institute Online site.

How Airplanes Work
www.howstuffworks.com/airplane/htm
Great science of flight explanations, diagrams, and detailed information on modern airplane components.

How We Made the First Flight
www.aero-web.org/history/wright/wright.htm
Read about how the Wright brothers invented the airplanes, in Orville's own words.

Milestones of Flight Gallery
www.nasm.si.edu/galleries/gal100/gal100.html
See the original 1903 Wright "Kitty Hawk" Flyer on this Smithsonian National Air and Space Museum Web site.

To Fly Is Everything ...
invention.psychology.msstate.edu
This "Virtual Museum Covering the Invention of the Airplane" has lots of information as well as 3-D images of early airplanes.

United States Air Force Museum Online Galleries
www.wpafb.af.mil/museum
See many of the aircraft built and flown by the Wright brothers and other pioneers of early flight.

Wright Brothers Aeroplane Company and Museum of Pioneer Aviation
www.first-to-fly.com
An amazing Web site bursting with information and images of everything from replicas of the 1899 kite to 2003 celebration events. Start at the Museum Guide to get your bearings!

Wright Brothers Negatives Search
memory.loc.gov/pp/wriquery.html
You can browse images taken by the Wright brothers by subject heading or search for particular photographs at this Library of Congress Web site.

Wright Brothers Online Exhibit
www.hfmgv.org/exhibits/wright/default.asp
This Henry Ford Museum & Greenfield Village Online Exhibit covers the life and work of the Wright brothers.

The Wright Experience
www.wrightexperience.com
These folks have set out "to rediscover the Wright Brothers experimentation, discovery, and methodology" by reconstructing—and flying—all the brothers' gliders and airplanes. The Web site highlights their progress and what they're learning along the way.

Places to Visit

Aviation Trail
P.O. Box 633
Wright Brothers Branch
Dayton, OH 45409
(937) 443-0793 or (937) 225-7705
aviationtrailinc.org
The Aviation Trail is a self-guided tour along dozens of Wright brothers–and aviation–related sites in and near Dayton, Ohio. After calling or writing to request a map and pamphlet, you can follow the Aviation Trail markers to visit the Wright Cycle Company, the US Air Force Museum, Hawthorn Hill mansion, the Wright Brothers Memorial, Huffman Prairie Flying Field, Wright State University, the cemetery where the Wright family is buried, the Dayton-Wright Brothers Airport where a you can see a flyable replica of the first mass production airplane—the Wright B Flyer—and many other sites.

Carillon Historical Park
2001 South Patterson Boulevard
Dayton, OH 45409
(937) 293-2841
This outdoor museum includes Wright Hall, a building designed by Orville Wright to house the restored original 1905 Wright Flyer III and a replica of the Wright Cycle Shop where the brothers built the 1903 Flyer.

Dayton Aviation Heritage National Historic Park
22 South Williams Street
Dayton, OH 45407
(937) 225-7705
www.nps.gov/daav
This National Park Service park preserves the legacy of the Wright brothers. It includes four Dayton sites associated with the Wright brothers: the restored Wright Cycle Company building used from 1895 to 1897 and the adjacent Hoover Block building where the Wright printing business was from 1890 to 1895; the Dunbar House State Memorial, home of the African American poet Paul Laurence Dunbar; the Wright Flyer III at Wright Hall at Carillon Historical Park; and the Huffman Prairie Flying Field.

Henry Ford Museum & Greenfield Village
20900 Oakwood Boulevard
Dearborn, MI 48121
(313) 271-1620
www.hfmgv.org
The Wright Cycle Shop where the brothers built the 1903 Flyer and the family house at 7 Hawthorn Street were moved from Dayton to Greenfield Village in 1937. Today they're part of the Henry Ford Museum and open to the public.

Smithsonian National Air and Space Museum
6th Street and Independence Avenue, SW
Washington, DC 20560
(202) 357-2700
www.nasm.si.edu
The world's first airplane, the 1903 "Kitty Hawk" Wright Flyer is on display here in the entryway. The world's first military airplane, the 1909 Wright Signal Corps Flyer, and the 1911 Wright Vin Fiz, the first airplane to fly across the United States, are also at the National Air and Space Museum.

United States Air Force Museum
Springfield Pike at Gate 29B
Wright-Patterson Air Force Base
Dayton, OH 45433
(937) 255-3286
www.wpafb.af.mil/museum
The USAF Museum is the oldest and largest military aviation museum in the world. It features more than 300 aircraft and exhibits that take the visitor through the history of human flight from Icarus to the space station. The Early Years Gallery has replicas of the gliders, balloons, flyers, and airplanes of early flight pioneers such as Chanute, Langley, Curtiss, and Blériot. Wright brothers artifacts at the museum include the 1911 modified B Flyer, a replica of brothers' 1901 wind tunnel, and lots of memorabilia.

Wright Brothers National Memorial
Kill Devil Hills
1401 National Park Drive
Manteo, NC 27954
(252) 441-7430
www.nps.gov/wrbr
To commemorate Wilbur and Orville Wright's first flight, a 60-foot granite monument was erected atop 90-foot Kill Devil Hill and dedicated in 1932. Today there's also a museum with full-size replicas of the 1902 glider and 1903 Flyer, reconstructed camp buildings, and numbered markers that indicate the distance of each of the four flights that were made on December 17, 1903.

Books to Read

*Berliner, Don. *Before the Wright Brothers*. Minneapolis, MN: Lerner Publications, 1990.

*Braybrook, Roy. *The Aircraft Encyclopedia*. New York: Julian Messner, 1985.

Crouch, Tom D. *The Bishop's Boys: A Life of Wilbur and Orville Wright*. New York and London: W. W. Norton & Company, 1989.

Culick, Fred E. C., and Spencer Dunmore. *On Great White Wings: The Wright Brothers and the Race for Flight*. New York: Hyperion, 2001.

Deines, Ann, ed. *Wilbur and Orville Wright: A Handbook of Facts*. Eastern National, 2001.

*Freedman, Russell. *The Wright Brothers: How They Invented the Airplane*. New York: Holiday House, 1994.

Howard, Fred. *Wilbur and Orville: A Biography of the Wright Brothers*. Mineola, NY: Dover Publications Inc., 1987.

Jakab, Peter L. *Visions of a Flying Machine: The Wright Brothers and the Process of Invention*. Washington, DC, and London: Smithsonian Institution Press, 1990.

Jane, Fred T. *Jane's Historical Aircraft, 1902–1916*. Garden City, NY: Doubleday Press, 1972.

Johnson, Mary Ann. *A Field Guide to Flight: On the Aviation Trail in Dayton, Ohio*. Dayton, OH: Landfall Press, 1996.

Kelly, Fred C. *The Wright Brothers*. Mineola, NY: Dover Publications Inc., 1989.

Macaulay, David. *The Way Things Work*. Boston, MA: Houghton Mifflin, 1988.

Montgomery, M. R., and Gerald L. Foster. *A Field Guide to Airplanes of North America*. New York: Houghton Mifflin Company, 1992.

*Nahum, Andrew. *Flying Machine*. New York: Alfred A. Knopf, 1990.

*Old, Wendie C. *The Wright Brothers: Inventors of the Airplane*. Berkeley Heights, NJ: Enslow Publishers, Inc., 2000.

*Parker, Steve. *The Wright Brothers and Aviation*. New York: Chelsea House, 1994.

*Reynolds, Quentin. *The Wright Brothers: Pioneers of American Aviation*. New York: Random House, 1981.

*Sobol, Donald J. *The Wright Brothers at Kitty Hawk*. New York: Scholastic, 1989.

Spangenburg, Ray, and Diane K. Moser. *The Story of Air Transport in America*. New York: Facts On File, 1992.

*Sproule, Anna. *The Wright Brothers: The Birth of Modern Aviation*. Woodbridge, CT: Blackbirch Press Inc., 1999.

*Stacey, Tom. *Airplanes: The Lure of Flight*. San Diego, CA: Lucent Books, Inc., 1990.

Wright, Orville. *How We Invented the Airplane: An Illustrated History*, edited with an Introduction and Commentary by Fred C. Kelly. Mineola, NY: Dover Publications Inc., 1988.

Wright, Wilbur and Orville. *Miracle at Kitty Hawk: The Letters of Wilbur and Orville Wright*. Fred. C. Kelly, ed. New York: Farrar, Straus and Young, 1951.

Wright, Wilbur and Orville. *The Papers of Wilbur and Orville Wright*. Marvin W. McFarland, ed. New York: McGraw-Hill, 1953.

*These books are recommended for young readers.

Videos

The Wright Stuff (American Experience). PBS Video, 1996.

Wilbur & Orville: Dreams of Flying (Arts & Entertainment Television Network: Biography). A&E Home Video, 1994.

The Magic of Flight (IMAX). Image Entertainment, 2000.

A reproduction of the Curtiss 1911 Model D Type IV pusher on display at the United States Air Force Museum. Curtiss's airplane was the second military airplane purchased by the U.S. Army Signal Corps, the Wright Signal Corps Flyer being the first.

Index

SEDGWICK MIDDLE SCHOOL
LIBRARY MEDIA CENTER
WEST HARTFORD, CT 06107